The M⦿DERN C⦿UPLE'S MONEY GUIDE

D0979803

Lesley-Anne Scorgie

The MODERN COUPLE'S MONEY GUIDE

7 Smart Steps to Building Wealth Together

DUNDURN
TORONTO

Project editor: Kathryn Lane
Copy editor: Natalie Meditsky
Printer: Webcom

Cover and interior design: Laura Boyle
Cover image: © iStockPhoto.com / AntonBalazh
Back cover image: Glen Co. Photography

Library and Archives Canada Cataloguing in Publication

Scorgie, Lesley-Anne, author
The modern couple's money guide : 7 smart steps to building wealth together / Lesley-Anne Scorgie.

Includes index.
Issued in print and electronic formats.
ISBN 978-1-4597-2977-3 (paperback).--ISBN 978-1-4597-2978-0 (pdf).-- ISBN 978-1-4597-2979-7 (epub)

1. Couples--Finance, Personal. I. Title.

HG179.S3525 2016   332.0240086'55   C2015-908789-9
                                                    C2015-908790-2

1 2 3 4 5   20 19 18 17 16

 Conseil des Arts   Canada Council
du Canada   for the Arts

We acknowledge the support of the **Canada Council for the Arts** and the **Ontario Arts Council** for our publishing program. We also acknowledge the financial support of the **Government of Canada** through the **Canada Book Fund** and **Livres Canada Books**, and the **Government of Ontario** through the **Ontario Book Publishing Tax Credit** and the **Ontario Media Development Corporation**.

Care has been taken to trace the ownership of copyright material used in this book. The author and the publisher welcome any information enabling them to rectify any references or credits in subsequent editions.
— J. Kirk Howard, President

The publisher is not responsible for websites or their content unless they are owned by the publisher.

Printed and bound in Canada.

VISIT US AT
Dundurn.com | @dundurnpress | Facebook.com/dundurnpress | Pinterest.com/dundurnpress

Dundurn
3 Church Street, Suite 500
Toronto, Ontario, Canada
M5E 1M2

Contents

Introduction

Besides infidelity, the fastest way to kill an intimate relationship — whether you're straight or gay, religious or agnostic, married or cohabitating — is to not be aligned with your partner regarding money — how to make it, spend it, grow it, and save it.

That's right! Money issues are indifferent to your age, gender, sexual orientation, life stage, and upbringing. And despite the material wealth and bright smiles we see on the outside, money issues affect rich couples, poor couples, and those in between.

Sadly, financial incompatibility is the leading cause of separation and divorce in North America — which is a complete shame, because it's avoidable.

> Money issues are indifferent to your age, gender, sexual orientation, life stage, and upbringing.

But when couples are pulling in opposite financial directions, they won't reach their financial, personal, and professional goals. This results in hurt feelings, major damage to a couple's financial progress, and in so many cases, complete relationship breakdown.

As partners, we do our best to love, protect, and uplift our life mates. But far too often we downgrade the importance of financial security below that of travel adventures, weddings, new houses, cars, careers, and starting a family. Sure, these are awesome and deeply fulfilling dreams, but without financial security as the foundation upon which to build these dreams, you'll become a slave to your loan, credit card, and mortgage payments.

Can you imagine how stressed and unhappy you would be if you and your partner ran the hamster wheel of debt for decades, never making any financial progress? Well, welcome to the lives of so many unhappy couples who are barely affording their lifestyle and blaming each other for being where they are. You know these people. They're house rich and cash poor. They're driving Land Rovers when they still have a landlord.

In contrast, the happiest couples are thought to be those who have high financial compatibility and work toward common goals. These couples make the most of what they have rather than focus on what they don't have. And many of them aren't considered "wealthy" just yet — but they're well on their way to financial success.

No, money can't make you and your partner happy. But having it, along with a mutual commitment to a financial plan for the future, opens doors for couples. Without money, you and your partner must accept your circumstances — both good and bad — rather than choose what's best for your future.

Think of it this way: Let's say you and your spouse are in your early 30s and are without children. You make a combined income of $70,000 and are working hard to save up to move to France. In France, you will both retrain for new careers — you as a chef and your spouse as a restaurateur. After five years of extremely frugal living and both working second jobs, you reach your savings goal of $60,000 together. You rent out your home on a two-year lease, purchase plane tickets to France, and off you go. When you and your spouse complete your training, job offers, as well as offers to finance your very own restaurant, come pouring in. Based on these preliminary offers, it appears that your combined income will be double what it used to be. You have many choices and agree to build a solid plan for your future.

On the other hand, imagine you and your partner are in your early 40s and have two children. Your combined income is $175,000, but you can't seem to control your spending. As the years pass, your debt load increases. Sure, your family "looks the part," driving nice cars and living in a fancy house, but you're strapped and can't afford anything but your mortgage, credit card, and car payments. Soon enough, after a brief period of unemployment, you're behind on your monthly payments and creditors begin calling. You and your partner start having fierce arguments — worse than in years past — about money. In this situation, your choices are limited. Your family either repays what it collectively owes, which you can't afford to do at the moment, or you'll lose your material possessions.

Having money helps you and your partner create higher-quality options for your future. And that's why smart couples take the time to build a plan to achieve financial success.

ONE-SIZE-FITS-ALL DOESN'T FIT

There isn't a prescribed one-size-fits-all financial plan for couples. "Financial success" is defined and created by you. And you'll know you've achieved it when you can choose what you want for your life.

Financial success for one couple could mean retiring at age 65 with $1.5 million in the bank, a home without a mortgage, and nice cars parked in the driveway. For another couple it could mean living and working abroad, building up a small, but sustaining, amount of retirement savings. The second couple would likely define financial success as having seen the world, whereas the first couple would define it as having enough to enjoy a luxurious lifestyle in retirement.

Neither couple's vision of financial success is better than the other's. As long as each couple has a plan and both partners work as a team, both couples will accomplish what they set out to do … and be happy in the process.

The Modern Couple's Money Guide will help you and your partner develop the skills to create a strong foundation upon which you can build *your own* version of financial success.

PUT THE PAST WHERE IT BELONGS

Starting today, you and your partner get to choose how you want your future to shape up, regardless of where you came from, your current bank balance, whether you're a spendthrift or ridiculously wealthy. If you choose a healthy attitude toward money management, meaning that you use money as a tool to build your dreams, not to accumulate copious amounts of debt for a lifestyle you can't afford, your financial foundation will become stronger, and you'll be happier.

Certainly we have all had experiences that negatively impact our attitudes and beliefs about money. But don't let the past be a barrier to creating a great future for you and your partner.

My early experiences with money, for example, were a mix of good and bad. By all accounts — and sociological statistics — I probably shouldn't even be writing this book. But rather than letting the financial challenges of my upbringing dictate my financial future with my life partner, I let them fuel my passion for building financial success.

You can do the same — leave the past in the past, especially if it's likely to have a negative impact on your future. Just learn from it. This may mean forgiving your partner for being financially irresponsible, setting healthy financial boundaries, or dramatically altering behaviours that are counterproductive to making progress on your money.

For example, you may have had a very luxurious lifestyle in a previous relationship. Perhaps you and your partner brought home a combined income of $750,000 annually. Fancy clothes, cars, electronics, trips, and houses were literally at your fingertips. But, for whatever reason, the relationship didn't work out. Now you're with your new love and have a fraction of the resources. He or she is a part-time fitness instructor, and you've transitioned into a lower-stress role as a marketing coordinator, versus your prior role as a marketing director. Your new household income is $90,000.

Is it fair to be upset with your new partner for not making as much as your previous partner? No, of course not! Your new partner is a different person with a different career altogether.

Is it wise to carry on spending as if you still had access to a $750,000 annual income? No, that would be foolish and would cause you and your partner financial hardship.

Is it fair or wise to fantasize about the material possessions you used to have? No. Living in the past will make you resentful about your current situation and it won't change your future. The only thing that will is learning from it.

When I was growing up in Toronto, Edmonton, and Calgary, my parents had very little money due to job instability, debt, and poor financial skills. As a family of five, we lived at the government-deemed poverty line for well over a decade. A small income of $24,000 per year put food on our table, a roof over our heads, transit passes in our hands, and clothing on our backs — second-hand, of course. As a result, we were forced to live a frugal and fun life, wasting nothing. I never had new clothes, shoes, bikes, or school supplies until I could afford to buy them myself with the earnings from my own part-time job in my teenage years.

Numerous times throughout my childhood, my parents would take my brother, sister, and me to the grocery store or Walmart, and load up the cart. When it came time to pay, they didn't have enough money. So we would go home empty-handed, and in some cases, hungry. Not surprisingly, on those days my parents would argue about their money situation; the three of us children could overhear from adjacent rooms. Like clockwork the next day, my mother or father provided my siblings and me a "what-not-to-do" lesson in money management. "Learn from us and don't repeat our mistakes" was the core message.

My parents ultimately divorced after years of financial, personal, and professional misunderstandings. They were on different financial pages and had been for years.

From watching my parents, I learned early on that money issues in relationships are rarely just about money. Often it's the "meaning" (attitudes and beliefs) behind the mismanagement of money that drives a wedge between couples. For example, one partner might feel the other was being selfish when purchasing an expensive television without consulting the other. Or, as in the case of my parents, clear financial boundaries were never established and resentment built steadily between them.

I was fearful of never having enough, just like my parents, and of failing in my own marriage. But rather than letting these negative experiences shape my future, I took them to heart, channelled my fear into motivation, and created a strong financial foundation.

I reprogrammed myself and the relationship I had with money so that it wouldn't destroy the relationship I have today with my intimate partner.

You and your partner can do the same and create a happy future.

Don't let past negative financial experiences, attitudes, and behaviours dictate your future.

THREE PILLARS FOR SAVVY COUPLES

Savvy modern couples take a three-pillared approach to building their lives and financial security together. They focus on strengthening their financial, personal, and professional lives.

When these pillars are strong, they are the foundation that supports a couple's future. This in turn allows them to achieve their full financial potential while feeling happy in the process. When any of these pillars are weak, a couple's foundation is weak, and it's hard to build a lasting structure on a cracked foundation.

Think of it like this: If one partner is a spender and compromises the couple's retirement savings because they bought too many handbags or car accessories, that will cause stress in the relationship. Stress impacts personal happiness and productivity at work. When a couple supports and respects each other's career aspirations, their collective income will grow, which strengthens their finances and generates better options for their future.

Or think of it like this: If a rich couple defines themselves by their wealth, rather than focusing on building a healthy relationship with each other, their friends, and their family, they'll push each other and their social circle away. Regardless of their bank balance or career success, they'll be miserable.

With so many competing priorities for your time, talents, and resources, it can be a challenge to place equal emphasis on your financial, personal, and professional success. But rich couples do — and so should you.

FROM BROKE TO OPRAH

At the age of 17 I was fortunate enough to meet one of the most influential women in the world — Oprah Winfrey. I was featured on her show in an episode called "Ordinary People, Extraordinary Wealth." I was one of a few guests sharing their financial secrets with more than 20 million viewers! My story stood out among those of the other guests primarily because of my young age, passion for financial literacy, and high bank balance.

I was on track to be rich — and able to retire, if I wanted — by the age of 30.

Coming from a low-income household inspired me to earn and save my money early on so I wouldn't have to experience the same hardships as my parents. From age 10 to age 14, I purchased Canada Savings Bonds with my birthday money every year.

I worked two flyer routes, babysat, sold lemonade, and picked weeds to earn money that I saved in a savings account until I was legally allowed to work at the local public library at the age of 14. From that time, every dollar that made its way into my hot little hands was deposited into my growing mutual fund account.

Thankfully, I took my investing quite seriously as an adolescent and read up on my hobby between my shifts at the library — *MoneySense*, *Forbes*, *Fortune*, the *Globe and Mail*, the *Wall Street Journal*, *The Wealthy Barber*. What I learned in the pages I read, I shared with a very kind and patient bank manager who worked across the street from my home.

I asked questions. I made mistakes. I fixed my mistakes. I consulted my parents. I grew my knowledge.

Before long, I had accumulated more savings than my parents, and had nearly enough to pay for my own university education.

In grade 12, my financial savvy was noticed by one of my teachers. She and I had enjoyed many conversations about investing and how to engage my peers in starting to save early on. When the local newspaper randomly phoned my high school one day looking for stories of "odd or interesting" students, my teacher proudly put my name forward.

The newspaper published a front page article entitled "Whiz Kid," which was then syndicated across North America. Shortly thereafter, in February 2001, I received a phone call from a producer at *The Oprah Winfrey Show*. Oprah had read the article and wanted me on the show to share my story. The rest is history.

As you know, Oprah has a massive influence on the lives and careers of the people she touches. I'm grateful to her because she's the primary reason I was able to go on to write two bestselling books: *Rich by Thirty: A Young Adult's Guide to Financial Success* and *Well-Heeled: The Smart Girl's Guide to Getting Rich.*

The experience I had with Oprah, along with wise guidance from my mentors and family, has helped shape me as a person. It's also influenced my business, MeVest, which is an online money school that provides financial education through one-on-one money coaching, eLearning, and financial planning.

WHY COUPLES MATTER

I care about improving financial literacy for couples because strong couples build strong families, communities, and workplaces. They are happy. They are inspirational.

But in my work as a professional speaker and the founder of MeVest, I've noticed a disheartening trend among 30- to 50-something couples. Most fight about money regularly because they don't know how to navigate difficult money conversations and they lack the skills to establish a strong financial foundation. Without major intervention, nearly half of these couple will end up negotiating separation agreements or signing on the dotted line of their divorce papers.

I full-heartedly believe that money matters don't have to continue destroying relationships. Instead, money can be used as a tool to help couples achieve their goals and dreams.

SEVEN STEPS TO FINANCIAL BLISS

If you're reading this book as a last-ditch attempt to get rich quick and save your relationship, I have bad news for you — money can't fix your relationship.

You and your partner need to create a strategy for your future and your money together. When you're aligned on where you want to go — even if it's just a mutual commitment to read this book at this point — *The Modern Couple's Money Guide* can show you how to get there by using these seven steps to build wealth together:

1. Get on the same page
2. Scrap your emotions and sort out your accounts
3. Curb overspending
4. Get the hell out of debt
5. Own the walls you live in
6. Invest like a pro
7. Design your master money plan

When combined, these steps will help you grow your net worth, which is the money you have left over once you subtract what you owe (liabilities) from what you own (assets). To build your net worth, you and your partner must increase your assets and reduce your liabilities (also known as debts). If you do the opposite, your net worth will shrink and eventually become negative. The stronger your net worth, the better the quantity and quality of your choices for the future.

The Modern Couple's Money Guide will teach you and your honey how to navigate through tough financial conversations without criticism, bickering, screaming, name-calling, shouting, or finger pointing. It also reveals the secrets of how financially successful and happy couples build a solid financial foundation — and how you can, too.

> The stronger your net worth, the better the quantity and quality of your choices for the future.

Building an incredible financial future with your life partner starts with open communication, respect, and a plan for the future. To reach your full financial potential, you must strengthen not only your finances but also your personal and professional life.

Enjoy the read!

CHAPTER 1
Get on the Same Page

Sarah called me a few years ago to tell me that she and her husband, Thomas, weren't doing so well. Through her sobbing, I learned that Thomas had started to move his stuff out. Sarah was hysterical — six years of marriage were crumbling beneath her.

After years of lavish living and serious overspending, Sarah and Thomas were up to their eyeballs in debt. Though they made a healthy combined income of $95,000, they were falling behind on car, credit card, loan, and rent payments. They shared one luxury vehicle, lived in a nice-sized condo in a hip area, shopped for expensive clothes, and took an exotic vacation each year. They had no savings.

For the majority of their marriage, Thomas had managed the finances. His philosophy was "live now, pay later." It wasn't until Sarah's credit card was declined at the grocery store that she had any clue they were maxed out.

Sarah quickly pulled her head out of the sand and confronted Thomas. Together they worked their way through stacks of unopened bills and letters from collections agencies. Learning they were $45,000 in debt and had no assets to their name meant long arguments. The blame game started and resentment built quickly.

Sarah interpreted Thomas's financial mismanagement as a demonstration of disrespect, lack of care, and misjudgment. Sarah also blamed Thomas for controlling their finances and thus trying to control her. She had blindly put her trust in Thomas's financial capabilities and, according to her, he'd broken that trust.

From Thomas's perspective, Sarah's lack of interest in their finances meant she didn't care much about their future. Often, he'd felt it necessary to make Sarah happy by spending money on expensive trips, meals, and clothes for her. He felt that she demanded this lifestyle. As well, she'd never helped out with the money management responsibilities.

The more they fought about the meaning behind their financial situation, the less they focused on actually resolving the problem.

I've seen couples just like Sarah and Thomas head straight for divorce court far too often. Their story is a common one: lack of healthy boundaries, such as spending limits, poor communication, and few skills to help them manage their money.

For Sarah and Thomas, a few simple lifestyle changes were necessary to alleviate the immediate financial pressure on their marriage. They had to sell their BMW, stick to a budget, and negotiate repayment terms with their lenders, all the while working to rebuild trust in each other. It took over a year, but eventually Sarah and Thomas got on the same financial page and stayed together.

MONEY AND EMOTION

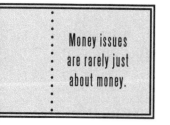

Money issues are rarely just about money.

Money issues are rarely just about money. Rather, they may represent much deeper issues such as control, independence, dependence, greed, trust, power, self-confidence, respect, and commitment. No wonder money breaks up so many relationships!

How you and your partner think, feel, and act about money is a reflection of your deeply rooted value systems. That's why spats over money boil down to the "meaning" of the financial choices each of you makes.

Take, for example, a couple in which one partner is working their tail off while the other is unemployed and not making a concerted effort to find work. The income earner may conclude that their partner is lazy, just like the rest of his or her family. Meanwhile, the unemployed partner may require a period of rest and regrouping after being fired or laid off from their recent job.

On the surface, it appears that this couple is struggling with one partner's unemployment. But issues of work ethic and rehabilitation are in play. To avoid relationship breakdown, both people in the couple need to understand and respect where the other is coming from.

START TALKING

You and your partner have developed attitudes toward money through childhood, school, culture, friends, careers, and trial and error. In some instances, you'll have had great role models in your parents. In others, your partner will have experienced a financially catastrophic event like bankruptcy or divorce. The following sections will help you and your partner think about your personal views on money and where they came from. I recommend you work through these questions together. Do not "pass go" until you've ironed out major discrepancies — trust me, they'll resurface if you don't.

If you and your partner fight a lot, you need to establish some ground rules. In fact, the simple Sparks motto, "I promise to share and be a friend" will do the trick (FYI — "Sparks" graduate to Brownies and then become full-fledged Girl Guides). That, and:

- Respect each other's views
- Be patient
- Be kind
- Be truthful
- No yelling

If you run into problems, get some help from a professional money coach, who will help you develop financial skill and work with you to design a financial plan for your future together, or you could even go to a relationship counsellor. You may find it easier to split this chapter up and address just one issue at a time.

DREAMS

Marty and Linda just got engaged. They're planning a wedding, a house purchase, future children, and the rest of their lives. Their biggest roadblock is that Marty just lost his job and the economic forecast isn't looking too hot for his line of work. Linda currently works to support their lifestyle. But money is really tight and causing arguments between them.

Marty and Linda have some big, and very natural, dreams for their life together. But with every dream come the hurdles and challenges associated with accomplishing it — in their case, Marty's unemployment. Navigating through good and bad times is part of building a healthy relationship. That's why it's helpful to discuss your dreams, how you're going to make them happen, and the "what-if" scenarios. Don't just assume that you're both working toward the same goals. Start this conversation by addressing the following:

- Describe a day-in-the-life of "us" five, ten, and twenty-five years from now.
- Where do you want to live?
- When do you want to retire?
- Do you want to travel? If so, where to?
- What type of job(s) do you want to have?
- What types of activities are you involved in?
- Do you want to achieve something extraordinary?

How did you do? Are your dreams aligned? Don't worry if it feels like your dreams of owning a vacation home in Florida seem out of reach today. A rock-solid financial plan will be the compass you need to get there ... and will also be the gauge of how realistic your dreams are. I'll help you build your plan in chapter 11, Design Your Master Money Plan.

LIFESTYLE

At age 31 and 34, Becky and Chris (common-law partners) believe in the value of experiences and living life to the fullest. They travel regularly, shop, eat out, and participate in expensive activities. Becky makes $100,000 annually and Chris makes $75,000. They have minimal savings, but they have an extensive digital photo album showcasing their worldly travels.

The purpose of earning money is to support a lifestyle. If a person's lifestyle is above or below their earning capacity, they run a deficit (a negative bank balance) or a surplus (money left over after the bills are paid). Sadly, many people spend a great deal more than they earn, which is the primary reason that savings rates in Canada have dipped so low. Overspending is not only bad for your wallet but also hard on your relationships. It can limit your ability to achieve short- and long-term goals, and can cause frustration and friction.

It's imperative that you discuss your lifestyle expectations with your partner and whether they are reasonable given your current and projected incomes. Here are some questions to ask that will help guide your discussion:

- What type of home do you want to live in (a cabin in the woods versus a beautiful house in the suburbs versus a downtown condo)?
- What kind of car do you want to drive (no car versus a flashy sports car versus a minivan)?
- How much would you like to spend on entertainment, clothes, and travel every year ($200 versus $2,000 versus $20,000)?
- Now and in the future, what kind of expenses **can't** you live without (books, vacations, gym memberships)?
- Now and in the future, what kind of expenses **can** you live without (expensive shoes, golf games, dining out, a car)?

A discussion about lifestyle will assist in developing techniques (such as budgeting or automatic saving) that will support it. For example, you may share the desire to take a vacation every year. To make this happen, you could adjust your household budget and cut back on restaurant and entertainment expenses.

SPENDING

Carlos and Maria fight about Carlos's spending. What frustrates Maria is that he spends his entire paycheque on digital equipment: mobile devices, video games, computer accessories, and cameras. He doesn't save any money. Maria, on the other hand, saves her money and rarely spends on things for herself. She gets frustrated because she feels that Carlos is being selfish and not saving enough for their future. He gets frustrated because she is too frugal.

Spending behaviours can reflect much bigger issues such as selfishness, stinginess, carelessness, disrespect, and lack of joint decision-making. That's why it's important to set spending boundaries together. Without them, partners may feel violated. For example, if a couple has a joint bank account but doesn't have an agreed-upon budget, one person could make a major purchase (electronics, furniture, appliances) without consulting the other.

How do you spend money? What motivates you to spend? Some people are impulse shoppers. Others are extremely tight with their cash. Often you'll find that spending is habitual or that you do it to fulfill a need that goes beyond what the purchase offers. Work through the following questions together and give yourselves the opportunity to reflect on your own:

- Where do you get your spending habits from? Parents? Friends? Work colleagues?
- What do you like to spend money on? Why?
- What payment methods do you use to spend (credit card, debit card, or cash)?
- Have you ever made a big purchase and regretted it? If so, what did you learn from the experience?
- Do you have a budget? Why? Or why not?
- Do you have money left over every month or are you in overdraft?
- Have you or your partner hurt each other because of poor spending habits? If so, how have you resolved these issues?

The key with spending is to spend less than you make. Otherwise, you'll go into debt and there are many strings — both personal and financial — attached to debt. The primary tool you have to help get a handle on spending is a budget, and I'll show you how that works in chapter 3, Scrap Your Emotions and Sort Out Your Accounts.

SAVING

Xu is a saver. He's 41 years old, owns a home, has $20,000 sitting in his savings account and $60,000 in his Registered Retirement Savings Plan (RRSP). He's miffed because his partner, Roi, doesn't have an equal amount of savings. Xu believes that their both having the same amount of money represents like-minded thinking.

Wanting dollar-for-dollar financial equality with your partner is natural but it isn't always realistic; one person's financial circumstances can be quite different from another's. For example, Xu's partner, Roi, might be a young lawyer still weighed down by student loans. Roi's long-term income-earning potential as a lawyer is greater than his short-term student loan commitments. So, if Xu wants to be with Roi, he'll have to evaluate both the short- and long-term financial potential of his partner.

> More important than your respective bank balances are compatible views on money.

More important than your respective bank balances are compatible views on money. When you share a parallel perspective, your financial goals are likely to be similar, which means that together, your actions will be complementary and focused on supporting those goals. Talk through the following questions:

- What assets have each of you brought into the relationship (savings, real estate, a business)? What made you successful at building assets in the past?
- What financial "baggage" have each of you brought into the relationship (a settlement from a lawsuit, a loan from a business that went sour, student loans, bankruptcy, racked-up credit cards)? Have you agreed on a strategy to deal with the baggage?
- Have you been successful at building assets together? What strategies worked?
- Have you accumulated debt together? How did that happen?

If you're worried that your partner is a gold digger or simply has a drastically different financial picture relative to yours, speak to a family lawyer about legally protecting your assets.

DEBT

Charles has $60,000 in debt, including student loans and a vehicle loan. Rebecca, his girlfriend, owes $35,000 on an investment loan. The couple's total debt comes to $95,000. They are discussing getting engaged.

Some people are comfortable carrying large amounts of debt; others are not. Some perceive certain debts to be "worth it"; others disagree. These days, debt has become part of the average person's finances due to the increased costs of education and housing, and also because of lifestyle choices and the availability of credit. Our grandparents' generation had little access to credit, forcing them to save up and pay for things in cash, and, therefore, have less debt. Yes, they still had daily living expenses, but many of the expenses we have today (two cars, large homes, luxury vacations) were deemed unnecessary back then. Having to save up and pay for things in cash eliminated our grandparents' opportunity to overextend themselves — the "buy now and pay later" approach used by many people today. It's important to align your beliefs about what *is* and *is not* worth going into debt for.

> Debt has become part of the average person's finances.

Obviously, it's in your best interest to focus on getting rid of, first, bad debt (expensive debt for non-assets like a television purchased on a store credit card) and second, good debt (debt for assets like a home). But if you and your partner don't understand the root cause of your debt accumulation, you'll always be in debt. I'll walk you through the Crush It debt-reduction system in chapter 5 (see page 66), but in the meantime, to prevent frustration and resentment, you first need to discuss debt and agree on solutions with which both of you are happy.

- Did your parents carry a lot of debt?
- Have you carried a credit card balance for more than 60 days in the past 12 months?
- Do you wonder where your money disappears to after payday?
- Do you feel like you are living paycheque to paycheque even though you earn a healthy income?
- Does debt cause stress?
- What's worth going into debt for?
- What debt-reduction techniques have worked for you in the past?

From a legal perspective, you are not responsible for your partner's debts prior to your union. But debt taken on during the union is legally your responsibility. So if your partner defaults on a loan that was signed for while the two of you were in a legal union, you are responsible.

INVESTING

Lindsay invests 15 percent of her annual income by contributing to her RRSP and TFSA (Tax-Free Savings Account). She's very career-focused and wants to retire at age 45 with $2 or $3 million in investments. Currently, Lindsay is 25 years old and has $30,000 invested.

Financial experts suggest that today's 30- to 50-something couple will need approximately $2 million to support an average retirement income of $8,000 per month until the end of their lives. That may seem like a lot of money — $96,000 a year, in fact — but powerful forces of inflation are working against you. Assuming you are 40 years old right now, in today's dollars that's more like $50,000 a year. As a general rule of thumb, to allow for $1,000 per month retirement income, you need to have $250,000 in retirement savings to generate it.

Sure, there are programs like Old Age Security (OAS) and the Canada and Quebec Pension Plans (CPP and QPP, respectively) that you'll receive money from in your golden years, but that money will compose only a mere 20 percent of your income needs, so they can't be relied on as the sole source of your retirement income. Old Age Security is a modest income benefit paid out (or clawed back if you've earned above the threshold during your working years) to Canadians over 65 regardless of their employment history. Most Canadians who have worked throughout their lifetime also contribute to the Canada Pension Plan or Quebec Pension Plan. These funds are paid out in retirement as early as age 60, but there are limits to the amount of money paid out through both. Service Canada (servicecanada.gc.ca) has information on OAS, CPP, and QPP rates.

Successful investing is vital to your retirement saving, and you simply can't rely upon government support, a possible windfall inheritance, or the lottery to get you there.

Discuss the following questions with your partner:

- On a scale of 1 to 5 (1 being low knowledge and experience and 5 being high knowledge and experience), how confident an investor are you?
- Are you a low- or high-risk investor?
- How much do you invest each month?
- Do you invest with a particular strategy in mind?
- Do you have a financial adviser? If so, do you like having an adviser? Why?

There are many different views on investing. Some people like to take risks, others are more conservative. People have different timelines in mind when they think of retirement. A money coach or financial adviser can help navigate any investing challenges and questions you and your partner might have.[1] We'll dive into this subject in a big way later on in *The Modern Couple's Money Guide* (see chapters 7 to 10).

FAMILY AND FRIENDS

Colin spends a great deal of time with his family and close friends. His partner, Angela, enjoys this time as well. Every so often, though, it gets in the

---

1 A financial adviser is different from a money coach in that financial advisers can manage your investments and provide investment advice. A money coach, on the other hand, cannot manage your investments, nor provide specific investment advice. Rather, they focus on growing your knowledge on savvy investing strategies.

way of their time together and their
shared values. Angela feels that Colin is
heavily influenced by his friends' and
family's views on money, career, and lifestyle, which doesn't allow him to think
independently. Colin, on the other hand,
really appreciates having the support and
advice of those closest to him.

> Establish clear financial boundaries first with your partner, then with those closest to you.

According to a 2013 BMO Bank of Montreal survey, most Canadian
couples wish they'd talked more openly and received professional
financial advice prior to forming a permanent household. The majority of people received financial advice from their parents and friends.
Unfortunately, as in my own case growing up, rarely are these sources
of information qualified to offer financial advice. So, as you and your
partner create a financial plan for your future, try to understand what
financial role parents, in-laws, siblings, extended family, and friends
will play in your life. Consider the following:

- What lessons have you learned about money from your family or friends?
- Do you agree or disagree with the way your family or
  friends manage their money?
- How do you feel about teaching your own children about
  money? If you have children, what will you tell them?
- Do your family or friends expect financial support from
  you today or in the future?

When money mixes with family and friends there can be strange out-
comes. Establish clear financial boundaries first with your partner, then
with those closest to you.

CHARITABLE GIVING

Sir John Templeton was arguably one of the most successful investors of
all time. He was born in Tennessee in 1912 and graduated from Yale in

1934. In 1954, he established the Templeton Growth Fund. The fund was incredibly successful. A $100,000 investment in that mutual fund in 1954 would have grown to over $60 million today through the power of compounded interest and reinvested returns. Templeton was worth billions, but what is most interesting about his story is his community involvement. Even when he was making less than $50 a week a few years out of school, Templeton invested his time, talent, and money in worthy causes. In 2007 Templeton was named one of *Time* magazine's "Power Givers" because of his philanthropy. Through the John Templeton Foundation, tens of millions of dollars have been invested *yearly* in cutting-edge scientific, spiritual, and educational research.

Charitable giving has become an essential piece of any sound financial plan. In fact, through my research and work, I've concluded that philanthropy is one of the top four characteristics that wealthy people share (the others are spending wisely, multiple income streams, and investing for the future). Whatever motivation a philanthropist has, whether recognition, or altruism, there is a return on investment (ROI) for giving back. Typically, ROI is received through direct dollars paid to an investor as a reward for the risks he or she takes investing their money. However, if we revisit the traditional definition of the term, ROI includes expanded networks (people or businesses you are involved with), increased sales, promotions, job offers, publicity, and so on. When you give back, people pay attention, and you become a hero and a leader in giving.

Your views on charitable giving are important to discuss with your partner. Some people prefer to donate time. Others money. Still others don't believe in philanthropy at all. Iron out any discrepancies, as your views on charitable giving represent much more than just a simple donation. Here are some conversation starters for you and your partner:

- Do you believe in philanthropy? Why or why not?
- What philanthropic initiatives have you been involved in?
- How do you like to give (time or money)?
- What skills or dollars do you think you could offer a charity?

I'LL HAVE TO GO THROUGH IT

Do you remember the children's song called "We're Going on a Bear Hunt"? The lyrics are about kids going on a bear hunt and encountering obstacles, such as tall grass, a tree, and a river, along the way. At every obstacle, they chant, "We can't go over it, we can't go under it," and then they select the appropriate action such as "We gotta go through it."

When challenging financial conversations pop up between you and your partner, keep these lyrics in mind, which essentially say that you need to work toward an appropriate solution rather that trying to avoid the obstacle. As the song and real life would suggest, avoidance doesn't get you anywhere closer to your goals.

TEAM APPROACH

To begin planning a great financial future, you need to start on the same page and work toward your goals as a team. There's simply no room in any relationship for unilateral decision-making, especially with your money.

CHAPTER 2
The Drivers of Net Worth

Couples that make it, and are happy, have what I like to call "sticky glue" between them. It's the bond that keeps them together even when times are tough. What strengthens that bond is building toward common goals that make the couple's life better — things like family, travel, or a new career path.

Some of the strongest sticky glue between partners is financial security because that's what funds the future you and your partner want to create. When you don't have financial security, or are building your own versions of it independently of each other, you'll grow apart.

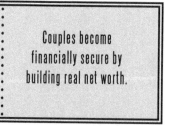

Couples become financially secure by building real net worth.

Rolling your eyes while reading this? Seriously, stop. I get that money matters can't dominate the core tenets of your relationship; love, respect, trust, and intimacy do. But you need to respect the power money has in your relationship. It's what rips people apart or pulls them together, and that's fact, not fiction.

Couples become financially secure by building real net worth. Net worth is the amount of money left over when you subtract your liabilities (what you owe) from your assets (what you own). If you own a home worth $250,000 and have investments worth $25,000, you have assets that total $275,000. But let's also point out that you owe $175,000 on your mortgage and have an outstanding consumer loan of $20,000. Your liabilities total $195,000. If you take your assets — $275,000 — and subtract your liabilities of $195,000, you have a net worth of $80,000.

NET-WORTH CALCULATION

Assets	$275,000
Liabilities	$195,000
Net worth (assets − liabilites)	$80,000

Your net worth is what you'll live off in retirement. It's what supports your dreams of travelling, getting your master's degree, or putting your kids through university. The greater your net worth, the more financial security you have.

Building net worth has absolutely nothing to do with how much money you make; it's about protecting and keeping the money you've worked so hard to earn. There are thousands of six-figure-income earning households that, in fact, have negative net worth because they've spent every dollar they have. Meanwhile, some of our clients at MeVest earn modest five-figure incomes and still manage to grow their net worth by thousands each year.

A good lot of people spin a web around their life to make it appear as though they have a high net worth. For example, one of our clients came to us driving a brand new Denali, having newly renovated her home, and wearing a huge two-carat rock on her ring finger. Shortly after she arrived for her appointment, her husband rolled up in a Mercedes-Benz and Hugo Boss suit. By all accounts, Gretta and Tom looked rich. But their MeVest money coach quickly discovered the wealth they were showcasing for their friends, family, and colleagues was financed entirely by credit cards and lines of credit. All tallied up, their net worth was negative $235,000, and they were ready to wring each other's necks.

In contrast, my savvy aunt and business mentor, a Toronto-based multi-millionaire interior designer, doesn't necessarily look the part by driving a flashy car and living in a mansion. She drives a practical used Audi station wagon, carries a stylish Roots bag, wears second-hand jewellery, and travels in economy class. Unlike Gretta and Tom, she can afford her lifestyle. According to my Aunt Marian, not living how rich people "should" live, with expensive material possessions that don't build wealth, has been critical to her financial success.

If you're guilty of keeping up with the Joneses, you now have a choice — to live like a millionaire or actually be one. And along your journey to building your net worth together, just remember — the Joneses are broke.

WHY BOTHER TRACKING NET WORTH?

Building your net worth starts with understanding where you are today. Your net worth is the number that we will focus on growing throughout this book. When you know where you are starting from, you can plan where you want to go. It's kind of like hopping on that dreaded scale in your bathroom to see how much you weigh. If the number disappoints you, then you make plans to change your fitness regimen and diet. Every week you weigh in to see your progress relative to where you started. If you find your weight heading in the opposite direction of where you want it to go, you can quickly course correct.

> When you know where you are starting from, you can plan where you want to go.

The same concept applies to tracking net worth. Today you might jump on the net-worth scale and be disappointed about where you are, like Gretta and Tom, and see that significant changes to your financial behaviours are required. Or you might weigh in and discover that you're satisfied with your net worth, and you simply need to keep up your regular financial-fitness regimen. On the opposite end of the spectrum from Gretta and Tom is my friend Sean, who paid off his mortgage in three years by sacrificing just about everything. Sean's net worth is high, but at the expense of furniture, worldly experiences, and relationships. His house and heart are empty and he'll need to make changes to his ultra-frugal financial habits to fill those voids.

The point is, when you take an honest look at your net-worth scale today, you can create a plan to grow your net worth through two actions. First, reduce debt like your car loan, mortgage, and credit card balances, and second, grow assets like your house, investments, or business.

Did you know that people who track their net worth either on paper, with an app, or by way of a spreadsheet make greater progress on their money than those who do not? That's because tracking your net worth adds an important layer of accountability to your net-worth goals. It forces you to face the financial music that you and your partner have created.

In his book *What They Don't Teach You at Harvard Business School*, Mark McCormack references a 1979 study on setting goals conducted with Harvard MBA students. Students were asked, "Have you set clear, written goals for your future and made plans to accomplish them?" At the time of the study, researchers found that 3 percent of the participants had clear, written goals, 13 percent had unwritten goals, and 84 percent had no specific goals. Ten years later, people with unwritten goals earned twice as much as those without any goals at all. Individuals with clear, written goals earned 10 times as much the other two groups combined!

When you track your net worth, you're more likely to accomplish the goals you've set to grow it. And if something goes off track, you can take immediate action to correct the situation.

JUMP ON IT

Ready to jump on the net-worth scale? Let's go!

If you're a busy person, or if you're using more than a simple bank account, keeping track of your money can be challenging. Many people have more than one bank or investment account, loan, credit card, or debit card. And when you layer on the fact that people often use multiple banks, passwords, and advisers, it's even more confusing. Wade through it by laying all your most-recent financial statements — either electronic ones that you've printed out or the hard copies you've received in the mail — on your kitchen countertop. Also sign into your accounts online so you can have your current balances on hand. It also makes sense to open up your wallet and lay your debit, credit, and store cards on the table just so you're not forgetting anything. Common statements include:

- Bank statements
- Mortgage statements/property value assessments

- Investment statements (from your bank, your RRSP, TFSA, or non-registered accounts)
- Credit card bills
- Loan and line of credit statements
- Pension statements
- IOUs (a rundown, handwritten if necessary, of money you owe to friends or family or that they owe you)

Once you have gathered your statements, begin inputting this information into a net-worth tracking tool. Not into designing your own spreadsheet? No problem, use Patrick and Morgan's Net-Worth Tracker (see opposite page) as a template. If you're uncertain which category to put a statement balance in, simply ask yourself this question: Do I need to repay this money? If the answer is yes, that balance is a liability.

Pay stubs, utility bills, and invoices for income are excluded from your net-worth calculation. They are used when budgeting instead (see page 48). Liabilities are different from bills in that liabilities are borrowed funds that must be repaid. Bills are paid monthly for goods or services — like your Internet or cable television service — delivered to you in a certain time frame. Bills should not be carried forward, whereas many liabilities, such as car loans and mortgages, are set up as regular payments over the course of many months. When a credit card balance isn't paid off every month, it becomes a liability rather than a regular monthly bill. (A budget tool can be used to track monthly bills and income. Budgets and tracking monthly expenses are discussed in chapter 3, Scrap Your Emotions and Sort Out Your Accounts, and chapter 4, Curb Overspending.) Assets, on the other hand, are owned by you and grow in value.

Tracking your net worth is a simple four-step process.

Step 1: Start by marking the date at the top of your spreadsheet.

Step 2: Record each asset or liability and its value.

Step 3: Add up your assets and liabilities.

Step 4: Subtract your total liabilities from your total assets, and voila — that's your current net worth.

Let's take Patrick and Morgan, both 45 years old, as an example. They own a home valued at $550,000 and have a mortgage of $315,000. Last year they did a renovation and financed it through a home equity line of credit, which has a balance of $40,000. Patrick has an RRSP through work and Morgan has a defined contribution pension plan through her employer. Patrick's RRSP is valued at $60,000 and Morgan's pension is worth $50,000. They have three children and a Registered Education Savings Plan (RESP) valued at $45,000. The couple struggles to pay off their credit card balances, which total $6,000 split evenly between two cards, every month. Patrick and Morgan's current net worth tallies to $344,000 when their total liabilities are subtracted from their assets.

PATRICK AND MORGAN'S NET-WORTH TRACKER

	Current value
Assets	
House	$550,000
Patrick's RRSP	$60,000
Morgan's pension	$50,000
RESP	$45,000
Total assets	$705,000
Liabilities	
Mortgage	$315,000
Home equity line of credit	$40,000
Credit card 1	$3,000
Credit card 2	$3,000
Total liabilities	$361,000
Net worth (assets – liabilities)	$344,000

Sometimes people don't have any assets or any liabilities. If that's you, simply put "0" as the value in the applicable category. If you don't know the exact value of an asset, like your home or a collector's item, you'll want to have an assessment done or do market research on comparable offerings. Sometimes your hard-copy bank or investment statements won't have the exact current value of an asset either. Simply call the institution where your bank account or investments are held and inquire about the current balance or check online.

Now it's your turn to try it. Work through your stack of financial statements one by one, placing the name and correct value in either the asset or liability column. As a reminder: your net-worth tracker is an entirely different tool from your budget. A net worth sums up your total assets and liabilities whereas a budget captures your monthly income and expenses.

How do you feel now that you know what your net worth is? A negative net worth isn't ideal because it means you owe more than you own. When you owe money, your options are limited — you either pay the money back or your lenders will harass you until you do. If you don't pay them back, your credit rating will be impacted in a negative way, making it harder for you to borrow money at affordable rates in the future. But don't worry if you're staring at a negative number. This book will show you how to increase your net worth and change that negative into a positive, which will allow you to have greater choices and flexibility with your future. However, when you have a positive net worth you can continue to build savings for retirement, start a business, put a down payment on a home, pay for your wedding, or invest in your education.

WHERE SHOULD OUR NET WORTH BE?

Almost every week I get asked "What should our net worth be?" The answer just isn't that simple, because it's based on what your goals are for the future. If, for example, you came to me and said you wanted to live on a beach in Bali and sell T-shirts for the rest of your life, I would tell you that you would need much less than someone who wants to take luxury cruises, play golf in warm climates, and shop for expensive jewellery in retirement. The person heading to Bali may need only $100,000 to live comfortably for the rest of their life, whereas the person heading down luxury lane would need closer to $4 million.

However, as a general rule of thumb, the average 30- to 50-something Canadian household will need approximately $2 million for retirement. So if you work that back, starting at the age of 25, and assume that as you age you'll make more and can afford to grow your net worth more aggressively through asset growth and debt reduction, you would need to reach the following net-worth milestones at these ages:

NET-WORTH MILESTONES FOR THE AVERAGE CANADIAN COUPLE

Age	Net worth
25	$0
30	$70,000
35	$165,000
40	$300,000
45	$465,000
50	$700,000
55	$1,000,000
60	$1,400,000
65	$2,000,000

Assumes a 6 percent rate of return.

Okay, I know that these numbers seem downright massive! But there are a few things that will work in your favour and push you much closer to achieving these targets.

1. **Compounded interest and reinvested returns:** The most powerful asset you have is time. The more time you have to save and invest your money, the more it will grow through the power of compounded interest and reinvested returns.

Compounded interest and reinvested returns mean that you earn interest and returns on your initial investment (the principal), which is then reinvested, allowing you to earn more interest and returns on it. So now you're earning interest and returns on the existing interest and returns. The more time you have to allow compounded interest and reinvested returns to actually *compound*, the more money you'll have in the end.

Think of it as piling rocks at the top of a mountain. You push the pile over the side of the mountain. On their way down, your rocks hit more rocks, which hit even more rocks. Before you know it, your little pile of rocks has started a landslide. That's how compounded interest and reinvested returns work: as time passes, your portfolio grows into something quite huge and all you needed to do was gather those initial rocks at the top of the mountain.

The longer you wait to invest your money, however, the less powerful compounded interest and reinvested returns are. Why? Because the less time you have, the less opportunity you give compounded interest and reinvested returns to compound themselves. Time is the magic ingredient that grows your money.

2. **Mortgage as a forced savings plan:** More than likely you will own a home in your lifetime. The act of repaying a mortgage forces you to reduce your outstanding mortgage balance, thus pushing your net worth higher every month. The only reason this would not work in your favour is if you borrow back the equity — typically through a low-rate line of credit or consolidation loan — you've put toward your house. I'll introduce the pros and cons of using lines of credit and consolidation loans in chapter 5 (see page 69).

3. **Inching your way to debt freedom:** Every month you will reduce your consumer debt (debt that isn't your mortgage) as long as you don't accumulate more. Again,

this builds your net worth through regular debt repayment. When you become debt-free, your cash flow will improve dramatically, allowing you to put more money toward assets.

4. **Automation:** Would you believe me if I said that you can build your net worth with your eyes closed? It's true. Through regular automatic contributions to your investment plans and the outstanding balances on your debts, including your mortgage, you can watch your net worth grow without having to do too much. Set up the transfers to come out of your chequing account on payday, before you've had the chance to spend the money.

HOW DO YOU WANT TO GROW?

Now that you've laid out your current net worth, it's time to give thought to how you'd like to see it grow.

Patrick and Morgan are starting with a net worth of $344,000. After discussing their goals for the next five years with their money coach, they learn that they are behind where they should be. Patrick and Morgan start to create a strategy to aggressively grow their net worth every month. The strategy requires Morgan to return to full-time work as a nurse. Currently, she works three days per week. Patrick will have to work toward becoming a foreman rather than a team lead at his roofing company to increase his income by at least 15 percent.

They've been big spenders for many years, and decide to cut back on out-of-country holidays, clothing purchases, and electronics for their children. They also agree to implement the Crush It debt-reduction strategy, which we'll discuss in chapter 5 (see page 66). Their goal is to have a net worth of $625,000 by the time they're 50, in five years.

Patrick and Morgan map out their plan by extending their net-worth-tracking spreadsheet over a five-year time frame. Then they calculate what each asset or liability balance needs to be in order to achieve their goals.

PATRICK AND MORGAN'S FIVE-YEAR NET-WORTH PLAN

	Current value	Year 1	Year 2	Year 3	Year 4	Year 5
Assets						
House	$550,000	$550,000	$550,000	$550,000	$550,000	$550,000
Patrick's work RRSP	$60,000	$70,000	$80,000	$90,000	$100,000	$110,000
Morgan's pension	$50,000	$60,000	$70,000	$80,000	$90,000	$100,000
RESP	$45,000	$46,000	$47,000	$48,000	$49,000	$50,000
Patrick's non-work RRSP	N/A	$1,000	$2,000	$3,000	$4,000	$5,000
Morgan's RRSP	N/A	$1,000	$2,000	$3,000	$4,000	$5,000
TFSA	N/A	$1,000	$2,000	$3,000	$4,000	$5,000
Total assets	**$705,000**	**$729,000**	**$753,000**	**$777,000**	**$801,000**	**$825,000**
Liabilities						
Mortgage	$315,000	$300,000	$275,000	$250,000	$225,000	$200,000
Home equity line of credit	$40,000	$30,000	$20,000	$10,000	$0	$0
Credit card 1	$3,000	$3,000	$0	$0	$0	$0
Credit card 2	$3,000	$0	$0	$0	$0	$0
Total liabilities	**$361,000**	**$333,000**	**$295,000**	**$260,000**	**$225,000**	**$200,000**
Net worth (assets − liabilities)	**$344,000**	**$396,000**	**$458,000**	**$517,000**	**$576,000**	**$625,000**

Patrick and Morgan have developed net-worth goals and "inked" them, which means there is a higher likelihood that they will achieve them than if they hadn't written them down. More important is that they have a *realistic* plan to make it all happen. The plan requires them to change their spending patterns and earn a higher household income.

Each couple's net-worth plan will be different from the next. Gretta and Tom, the couple with all the bling at the beginning of this chapter, would likely map out a plan whereby over five years they achieve debt freedom, bringing their net worth from negative $235,000 to $0. Still another couple, with a very modest income, could have a net-worth plan that brings them from $0 net worth today to $15,000 in five years. The point here is that your net-worth goals are yours and no one else's.

Take a stab at extending your net-worth plan over five years. Don't worry, the rest of this book will give you effective strategies to help make it happen, including advice on how to invest wisely, buy real estate, and pay down debt. But for now, outline your net-worth goals as realistically as possible. You can revisit and refine them later as you learn new financial strategies. Use Patrick and Morgan's Five-Year Net-Worth Plan (see previous page) to get started.

Congratulations! Setting some net-worth targets for yourself is the first step toward creating a rock-solid financial plan. I'll show you other important components of your plan in chapter 11, Design Your Master Money Plan.

FUEL FOR YOUR NET WORTH

You've probably figured this out by now, but your household income is the primary fuel for your net-worth growth. That means it's pretty important to protect and try to grow your income every year. When was the last time you got a raise or bonus? Could you be working for a different company that pays more? Could you start your own side business? As we move through the remaining chapters, think about how you can expand the size of your household income.

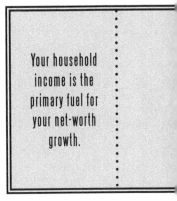

Your household income is the primary fuel for your net-worth growth.

MONITORING NET-WORTH GROWTH

The best way to monitor your net-worth growth is to periodically update your personal net-worth tracker. At a minimum, you should check in every six months. For example, in January 2017 you might be worth $25,000, and in June 2017, $30,000, and on and on. If you find you're getting off track, do some course correction and carry on.

Once you start implementing the principles discussed in this book, such as adopting the habits of truly wealthy people — and not those that just look rich but are actually broke — reducing debt, and growing assets, you'll see that net-worth figure start to grow. There's nothing more exciting than watching yourself get closer and closer to financial freedom.

CHAPTER 3
Scrap Your Emotions and Sort Out Your Accounts

Have you ever skied down a black diamond run with a blindfold on? Probably not — it's crazy dangerous and just plain stupid. So is allowing your partner to call important financial shots on your behalf.

One of my very first clients was a newly divorced woman, aged 40. During her 10-year marriage, she let her husband manage their investments. After her separation agreement was finalized, she had no idea how their money had been invested. As it turns out, her ex-husband was highly conservative and had kept the bulk of their money in guaranteed investment certificates (GICs) and cash, earning little interest. Meanwhile, my client would have been better off taking on more risk to grow her portfolio. But because she didn't get involved in the decision making around her investments, she missed out on a decade's worth of portfolio growth.

If you're guilty of deferring important financial affairs in your household to your partner, that needs to stop today! I don't care if your partner is better with money than you. This isn't the 1950s. Both partners have an equal responsibility to make savvy financial choices *together* — as a team. Whether money matters are your "thing" or not, you should take an interest in them to avoid finding yourself in a financial situation of which you weren't fully aware.

Consider the task of checking up on your personal finances like taking your car in for regular maintenance. If

> Consider the task of checking up on your personal finances like taking your car in for regular maintenance.

you take care of your vehicle, it will run smoothly and for a lot longer than if you were to neglect it. It's the responsible thing to do.

FINANCIAL CHORES

What financial tasks or responsibilities happen in your household? As a best practice, it's wise to swap these chores every few months so that both partners know how to do all the important financial tasks. You may find through this process that one partner is better at a particular task than the other. And it's okay to lean on each other's expertise, but both of you should be able to perform all of the financial chores required to run your home. Just imagine what a pickle you'd be in if your partner went into a coma and you'd never logged into your online banking.

Take 10 minutes to create a list of financial chores that are done in your home. For example:

- Bill payments
- Investing
- Online bank transfers
- Meeting with the bank for loans, mortgages, or credit cards
- Budgeting
- Buying a home, a car, or other big-ticket purchases
- Negotiating prices or interest rates

Once you've created a list, assign the tasks equally. Should you or your partner find that you're having trouble completing certain financial chores, help each other out or simply do a search on Google for best practices on subjects like budgeting, investing fundamentals, interest rate negotiation, or how to hire the right financial adviser.

Accounts

When couples get together, both partners have their own existing bank accounts, credit cards, loans, mortgages, and leases. Early in a formal union, couples face the choice of joining their finances or continuing to operate independently. Regardless of your personal views on this, stats show that neither approach is better than the other. It's completely up to the couple to decide what's best for them. And the great thing is that if you find sharing a bank account to be problematic, you can switch back to banking independently.

My grandmother and grandfather on my father's side were married in 1948. My grandmother was a book keeper in Toronto (until "quitting" work because she got pregnant) and my grandfather worked in the finance department of an electronics company for his career. They had separate bank accounts when they met and continued to maintain that system for over 60 years, until my grandfather passed away. Separate accounts were not a problem for them. They developed a household budget together, which my grandmother managed on a day-to-day basis, and they always discussed big financial decisions.

My grandparents on my mother's side managed their money in the opposite way. After returning from World War II with his blushing war bride, my grandmother, my grandfather set up their finances jointly. Chequing, savings, investments went in both names from the moment my grandmother landed on Canadian soil. My grandparents made financial decisions together, which is what helped keep them together.

The moral of these stories is that it really doesn't matter whether you and your partner join your accounts or not. As long as you plan your finances together, like a team, you'll be fine. But, if you plan them apart, like you're planning for different priorities that are not aligned, that's when you'll run into serious relationship and financial trouble.

I do have three tips, however, if you choose to keep your accounts separate.

First, I recommend that you keep each other apprised of what's happening with your day-to-day banking, investments, and other financial matters. This helps to ensure transparency.

Second, have a crystal-clear agreement about who is responsible for paying certain bills, like the mortgage, or making important contributions, like to your RRSPs by the annual deadline.

Third, in the event that something happens to one of you (death or a terrible accident), you need to have ready access to all of your partner's financial resources — and his or her will, but we'll get to that later on. One of my best friends' father passed away unexpectedly while the family was on vacation in Jamaica. She was only 10 years old at the time. Because the events around his death were suspicious, and her mother wasn't joint on his accounts and had nothing in her own name, she had to fight with the probate court system for over a year before seeing a single penny from his estate. Throughout that year she struggled to pay their mortgage and other bills.

There are many benefits to combining your chequing, savings, credit card, and investment accounts:

- You have fewer accounts to monitor and lower banking fees.
- You benefit from increased transparency in that you both have access to and can see all the account activities. This makes it easier to have an open discussion about what's happening in the accounts, create a budget, and manage accounting and taxes.
- In case of an emergency, both partners have access to all financial resources.
- If one person earns a much higher income, it can be shared easily.

There are also drawbacks to sharing accounts:

- When couples pool their incomes, it creates the perception that they have more money than before, which can quickly trigger overspending.
- Couples can get frustrated and may disagree with each other's spending patterns.
- If the relationship breaks down, there's a risk of one partner taking off with the financial resources. This would end up being settled later on in court, but it would cause a great deal of short-term financial pain.
- When you apply for credit in both names, you're evaluated on both your credit scores, and if one partner's score is bad, it'll affect the joint application.

To join or not to join — the choice is yours. Transparency is key.

Bills and Loans

Paying bills blows, but it is an inescapable fact of life. From a legal perspective, the person whose name is listed on the bill is the person responsible for paying it. And if the bills don't get paid, the billing companies will harass you at home and at work, and eventually report you to the credit reporting agencies (there are two in Canada, Equifax and TransUnion). These organizations monitor your credit management history and assign you a credit score. If you have a high score, it indicates that you are responsible with credit. When bills are not paid on time or in full, your credit score will be eroded and it will become difficult to get additional credit.

It's in your best interest to register the bills in the name of the person who will ensure they get paid on time and in full. It's very important to note that if your name is not on the bills, you do not build credit even if you live in the same house and have a joint bank account. So, if you want to build a positive credit record, put the bills in your name and pay them on time and in full.

Often, partners bring existing bills or loans into their union. For example, one person could have a $20,000 student loan while the other has no debt. Legally, you aren't held responsible for any debt assumed by your partner prior to your union — just the debt and bills accumulated during your union. But, in some form or fashion, you are responsible for everything because you have to live with your partner's cash-flow limitations.

Take, for example, Alicia. She has a massive line of credit of $90,000 from a business that she started a few years before meeting her partner, Max. The business went belly up and Alicia is stuck making payments of $900 per month on the line of credit. Max gets frustrated because Alicia's debt is preventing them from purchasing a larger home. Yet Max had nothing to do with accumulating the debt in the first place.

Alicia and Max's situation isn't uncommon and could easily lead to major fights. To avoid unnecessary tension, they'll have to create a plan to eliminate the line of credit as quickly as possible. The big question is whether Max should help Alicia out or let her pay off the debt alone. I can't answer that question for them because it's a personal choice. But what I can share is that the faster Alicia is free from her debt, the sooner Max and Alicia can get a larger home.

WHAT ARE YOU BRINGING TO THE TABLE?

If you're reading this book, it probably means you're already hooked-up. But Max and Alicia's situation is exactly the reason partners need to have a full understanding of each other's finances prior to making a commitment. Otherwise, whopping piles of debt, which have the potential to destroy your relationship, can quickly creep up on your household.

Regardless of how much you love and trust someone, you must understand both individuals' net worth. Unless you have a legal agreement stating otherwise, you share in each other's assets (the good) and liabilities (the bad) accumulated after your union is formally recognized. So it's good to know what financial commitments you'll eventually be responsible for. You should also know your partner's credit score, as it will factor into all your joint credit applications in the future.

If you haven't done so, I recommend discussing and showing your partner all of the assets and liabilities held in your name — credit card statements, mortgage statements, property value assessments, and investment statements — and seeing theirs. You'll then be able to determine each other's net worth (hint — use Patrick and Morgan's Net-Worth Tracker from chapter 2 as a template. See page 35). Also, pull your credit report and discuss it with your partner (credit reports are available through Equifax and TransUnion and you're entitled to a free one every year). A good friend of mine, Erica, married her husband not knowing he'd declared bankruptcy five years prior to getting hitched. It's been very hard on their marriage because they can't qualify for a joint mortgage or any additional credit.

This financial "tell-all" is best done over a glass of wine and some Lenny Kravitz.

BUDGETS

The purpose of a budget is to track your income and expenses over a month so that you can support both your long- and short-term goals. It is also a great tool to help set financial boundaries and accountability in a relationship. Under no circumstances should a budget be a unilateral decision — one partner telling the other partner what he or she can and cannot spend. In fact, in extreme cases, that's a form of financial abuse.

One of the primary reasons businesses and households go bankrupt is due to improper cash-flow management. In other words, they spend more money than is available and eventually run out. They clearly didn't have a budget, or they blew their budget out of the water. According to Thomas Stanley and William Danko's *Millionaire Next Door*, most self-made millionaires keep and maintain a meticulous budget. They know exactly what amount their household spends on food, clothing, shelter, entertainment, and in other spending categories. According to them, budgeting is one of the best tools a household can use to build net worth.

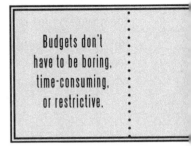

Budgets don't have to be boring, time-consuming, or restrictive.

Budgets don't have to be boring, time-consuming, or restrictive; rather, they are the opposite. They help you and your partner spend less of your time worrying about money and more time focusing on more important things in your life. Plus, you can build whatever you want into your budget — including fun. Without one, it's next to impossible to know where your money is coming from or going to.

Today there are hundreds of budgeting templates you can use. Access them through your bank's website, sites like mint.com, or Google Docs. You can even set up your own template using Microsoft Excel and the monthly budget template we'll walk through next. The tool doesn't matter, just so long as you have a budget and follow it. When you don't, that's when you'll fly off track.

Budget Basics

Marcus, 35, and Lydia, 33, manage their money carefully. Through joint decision-making and open communication, they're able to stick to a budget. They want to enjoy their life, and plan to retire at age 60. They have two kids in elementary school, work full-time, and have a mortgage and two cars. Marcus and Lydia plan to save more money for their retirement once the second car is paid off.

Let's drill into Marcus and Lydia's monthly budget. The first step when drawing up a budget is to identify all sources of income and record your net income, or income after taxes (effectively, what hits your bank account). Where does your money come from: employment (including contract work, freelance work, royalties), income from investments, government support, family support, spousal support, an inheritance? Identify all types of income. Below is an example of Marcus and Lydia's monthly income. Marcus is an insurance specialist and Lydia sells pharmaceuticals. Lydia also writes for a popular mommy-blog every month, which earns her a small side income.

INCOME

Income (after tax)	Average month
Marcus's paycheque	$2,500
Lydia's paycheque	$3,000
Lydia's freelance writing	$150
Total income	$5,650

Pretty straightforward, right? Mapping out your expenses can be a bit more difficult. Sure, it's easy to identify major expenses such as a mortgage payment, car loan, and RRSP contribution, but smaller expenses (coffee, drinks, lunches, movie rentals, and banking fees) are sometimes overlooked.

I recommend that every household go through the exercise of tracking every single expense for at least four weeks. Then you'll put together a spending summary. All you need to do is keep your receipts for four weeks — from the pack of gum purchased at your local convenience store to the tools you bought at the hardware store — and tally them up into categories like food, school fees, clothes, et cetera. A spending summary quickly reveals where your money is going — and the results may be a little shocking to you. Then you translate this spending into the ideal amount you'd like to spend in your monthly budget. For example, if you spent $550 last month on groceries, and that wasn't an unusual amount, you could budget to spend that same amount going forward.

Record your mandatory expenses first. These are things that you can't live without. Lydia and Marcus, for example, have their RRSPs, RESPs for their children, contribution toward their emergency fund, and mortgage payments in this category. Lydia and Marcus are using the "pay-yourself-first" strategy, meaning their financial future is so important to them that they tuck away money for themselves before anything else. This ensures they are prepared for retirement.

Secondary expenses follow the mandatory ones. These are the types of expenses you could live without if you absolutely had to. I like to think of them as the luxuries we like to have in our lives — the fun stuff. Secondary expenses are important because they tend to enhance our lives. Here's what Marcus and Lydia's expenses look like:

EXPENSES

Mandatory expenses	Average month
Marcus's RRSP contribution	$200
Lydia's RRSP contribution	$200
RESP contribution	$100
Emergency fund	$150
Mortgage	$1,200
Car loan	$350
Visa bill	$300
Groceries	$750
Heat	$150
Property tax	$200
Electricity and water	$175
Home and auto insurance	$225
Household maintenance	$100
Transit pass	$150
Vehicle fuel	$200
Clothing for the family	$250
Total mandatory expenses	$4,700

Secondary expenses	
Cell phones	$120
Internet	$65
Family gym membership	$120
Vacation savings	$150
Entertainment and fun money	$450
Total secondary expenses	$905
Total expenses	$5,605

The last thing you need to do with your budget is take your total income and subtract your total expenses. You'll then be able to see if you're spending more (deficit) or less (surplus) than you make each month. In Marcus and Lydia's case that's $5,650 minus $5,605, and they have an extra $45 kicking around after all their expenses, even the fun ones, have been paid.

You can customize your budget to your own situation. Budgets require balance and you need to reward yourself too. Just be reasonable with your spending. Rewards will be so much more meaningful when you've earned them through disciplined spending and have saved for them in advance.

Are you and your honey in a negative position each month? If so, or if you're simply not saving enough for retirement, that means you need to make changes to your budget and adopt the Frugal Fundamentals (see page 56).

According to *The Millionaire Next Door*, most millionaires have never paid more than $399 for a suit, $140 for shoes, or $235 for a watch. The majority drive older-model cars that they buy rather than lease. And they don't always live in super-fancy shacks!

No matter how much money you earn on an annual basis, if you don't learn how to keep it, just like wealthy people, you won't achieve financial freedom. That's right — it doesn't matter how much you earn, it's what you keep that counts. You could make $250,000 a year and, if you spend it all frivolously, in the long run you're no better off than the person who earns $25,000 a year and spends it all. So, let's be honest. If you're spending too much money (running a deficit), it's time to change your habits.

DON'T GET BLINDSIDED

A joint budget is one of the most effective tools available for you and your partner to hold each other accountable. But I still believe it is always a good idea to have some sort of financial independence. Save enough to take care of yourself and any emergencies or major changes in life circumstances you might face. Having access to your own savings provides greater independence, choices, security, and stability. No, this isn't about hiding money from your partner. It's about ensuring you have some financial resources if and when you need them.

> No matter how much money you earn, if you don't keep it, you won't achieve financial freedom.

SCATTER NO MORE

As a part of getting your financial house in order, I highly recommend you streamline your accounts. More times than not, I see couples struggling to figure out where all their money is — multiple chequing and savings accounts, investments with various brokerages, mortgages, loans, and lines of credit with different lenders. Do your financial self a HUGE favour and corral your accounts into one or two service providers. It's easier to track, you'll pay far less in service fees, and your leverage to negotiate for better rates goes up exponentially when you have more business with your chosen financial institution.

Yes, this takes valuable time. But it's time well spent. Fill out the necessary transfer and account-closure forms and your life will become easier and more organized.

CHAPTER 4
Curb Overspending

The cycle of overspending works like this: you spend more than your paycheque so you use your credit card to tide you over, when you get paid again you pay off what you spent the previous month but then you have no cash left for the current month. You promise you'll cut back your spending but life happens and you spend more than your paycheque, you use your credit card to tide you over, you get paid, you pay off what you spent the previous month but then you have no cash left for the current month ... and on it goes.

To get off this budget-busting merry-go-round you have three options: borrow money, increase your income, or reduce your spending. Borrowing money is a bad idea because it just deals with the symptoms rather than the actual problem, which is overspending. Increasing your income can be helpful, but overspenders typically end up spending their extra income. Reducing your spending and learning to live frugally gets to the root of the overspending problem. It forces you to re-evaluate your priorities, form different habits, and work hard toward permanently improving your financial situation.

Perhaps you're overspending each month in a moderate way — by $50 to $500. You can make small adjustments to your spending to help improve the situation. First, it's really important to recognize that many of the inexpensive things you spend money on each day can add up to quite a significant amount in a month, a year, and a lifetime.

Grabbing breakfast each weekday morning, for example, can really add up. If, for example, you buy a large coffee and a bagel for four dollars five days a week for 52 weeks each year. In one week, that adds up to $20 ($4 × 5 days). Over a year, it equals $1,040. If you did this throughout your working career, from age 25 to 65 (when you retire), you'd end up spending approximately $330,000 on coffees and bagels (if this amount is compounded at 8.5 percent annually)! If you made a change to your spending pattern and bought a coffee and bagel for four dollars *three* days a week, you'd spend $12 a week ($4 × 3 days). Over a year (52 weeks), that equals $624. If you tried this three-day-a-week spending pattern throughout your working career, from age 25 to 65, you'd end up spending approximately $200,000 on coffees and bagels (if this amount is compounded at 8.5 percent annually). As you can see from this example, simply cutting back your consumption slightly can save you hundreds of thousands of dollars in the long run.

Get your priorities straight and be ruthless about sticking to them.

To further illustrate, if you bought lunch every weekday throughout your working career for eight dollars each day, it would add up to $40 each week ($8 × 5 days), and $2,080 in a year. Compounded throughout your working career at 8.5 percent annually, this equals more than $650,000 in lunches! If you simply cut back your lunch spending to three days per week, you'd spend $24 each week ($8 × three days) and $1,248 in a year. Compounded throughout your working career at 8.5 percent annually, this would equal approximately $400,000 in lunches. You'd end up saving more than $250,000 by making a simple change to your spending pattern.

Just imagine how much more financial freedom you'd have if you chose to invest the difference of that money rather than literally ingest it. I recognize that you still need to eat and drink and that there are costs associated with doing that. But traditionally, making your coffee at home and packing your lunch is cheaper than eating out at coffee shops and restaurants, which charge a large margin on their sales.

Want more tips on how to cut out the small stuff? I call these the Frugal Fundamentals:

FRUGAL FUNDAMENTALS

Get Ruthless

Get your priorities straight and be ruthless about sticking to them. If retirement savings are more important than seeing a movie once a week, stop seeing movies once a week and plough that money into your RRSP instead. Ask yourself whether you really *need* the item in question or if you just *want* it.

If you really, *really* want something, especially something big like a TV or new car, try waiting a week or two before buying. You might reconsider.

Get Active

- If you're used to driving, take public transit, carpool, walk, run, bike, or in-line skate instead.
- Rather than shopping or spending money on costly entertainment, get active. Go running, biking, walking, skating, or hiking; do yoga outside; play football or baseball; walk the dog; play with your kids; or create some romance with your partner.

Get Healthy

- Cook at home rather than eat at restaurants.
- Stop drinking pop and juices.
- Try cutting back on meat — vegetarian dishes are often cheaper to prepare and highly nutritious.
- Stop smoking and drinking.
- Pack a lunch and make your coffee at home.
- Buy food in bulk, especially if you've got a family — the bigger the package, the more you save.
- Buy locally grown food or shop at a farmers' market — prices might be lower than at a grocery store especially when you purchase food in-season.

- Exercise at home or outside — YouTube has just about any exercise routine you can imagine.

Get Cheap Entertainment

- Borrow books, magazines, movies, and music from your local public library.
- Sign your kids up for free programs sponsored by your local library, municipality, and school board.
- Watch movies at home, use two-for-one coupons, or go to a discount theatre.
- If you like date nights, try going for a coffee rather than dinner, or a walk rather than a drive. Test out a recipe at home, watch old flicks, or spend more time chatting.
- If you like to socialize, have friends over rather than go out. You can host a potluck, play board games, watch the game, or chit-chat.
- If you like to travel, travel close to home. Drive to a destination rather than fly. Look for travel specials and take advantage of travel rewards programs.

Get Negotiating

- Always ask for a discount (negotiate everything). Remember, if you don't ask, you don't get.
- Always buy things on sale. If it's not on sale, find out when it will be or check the Internet for coupons.
- Negotiate cell phone, cable, and Internet plans.
- Call your bank or financial institution and negotiate the interest rates on all of your loans and credit cards.

Get a Bargain

- Buy used through local classifieds websites such as Kijiji, eBay, and Craigslist, or shop garage sales, estate sales, and auctions.

- Check out second-hand stores for cool clothes, jewellery, and accessories.
- Always look for sales and discounts. Going-out-of-business sales can have incredible bargains.
- Wherever you shop, check to see if they have a free rewards program. Everyone likes free stuff!
- See whether you can get a rebate on your purchase. Government websites and well-established couponing websites showcase popular rebate programs. For example, if you're going to renovate your home, retrofit with energy-efficient hot-water tanks, windows, faucets, and doors. There are thousands of environmental rebate programs throughout North America.
- Check to see if your employer or the government offers any coverage or subsidies for things such as child care, fitness expenses, and health and dental expenses. Check out the benefit-payments section of the Canada Revenue Agency website (cra-arc.gc.ca/ndvdls-fmls/menu-eng.html) and check with your employer's HR department.

Remember: A deal that you can't afford is never a good deal.

Get the Minimum

- Pare down your purchases. Buy the car without the sunroof. Buy the gym membership without the personal trainer. Split the football season tickets with a friend. Fly economy rather than first class. Stay in the standard room rather than the luxury room.
- Buy generic-brand products rather than brand-name.

Get Environmentally Friendly

- Save on utility bills by washing laundry in cold water, turning the temperature down a few degrees in your house, turning the lights out, and properly sealing your doors and windows.

- Reuse or recycle old things like plastic bags and containers.
- Share hand-me-downs with family, friends, and neighbours.
- Ensure that your car is well maintained; it will create less pollution and last longer.

Get Smart about Maintenance

- Do your own maintenance. Many people pay others to do things they can do themselves: yard work, home maintenance, car maintenance, housecleaning, washing, and ironing. You could even start your own small business doing things others don't want to do.

Get Rid of Excess Credit

- The more credit cards you have, the more they occupy your available credit so keep only one: the one with the longest history, smallest annual fee, best customer service, and lowest interest rate. Some cards automatically give you an annual credit limit increase. Instruct your credit card company to keep the limit at a level that you can afford, such as $5,000.
- If you struggle with credit card temptation, get the cards out of your sight! Cut them up, bury them in the backyard (I'm not joking), or stick them in a resealable bag, fill the bag with water, and put the whole package in the freezer. By the time your cards have thawed, you'll have had a chance to think twice about making that "must-have" purchase — and don't bother trying to hammer the ice; that will just wreck the cards.

By no means am I suggesting that you cut back so severely that you aren't able to have fun anymore. But if you and your partner struggle with overspending, try implementing just a few of these ideas *and* holding each other accountable to your budget. The rewards of adjusting your consumption far outweigh the costs of overspending and accumulating debt.

FINANCIAL HEMORRHAGING

If you're overspending in a major way — more than $500 per month — your financial ship is sinking fast and drastic changes to your spending are required. Things such as unemployment, an accident, or just plain overspending might be the cause of such circumstances. If you're really in a pinch and need to drastically cut back spending, implement the strategies above, but also consider the following:

- Downsize your home or rent for less.
- Get a roommate or rent out your basement.
- Lease out storage or a parking space.
- If your family owns two vehicles, sell one and share the other.
- Sell luxury items online.
- If you make a purchase, buy used.
- Get another job. If you like sports, for example, consider refereeing a few games each week. Or work the night shift security desk at a nearby condominium.
- If you have a hobby (decorating, writing, photography, bodybuilding), start a small business to increase your cash flow.

Drastic financial challenges call for drastic financial changes. Making them is generally uncomfortable, but you're better off making the changes quickly. If you wait, your financial circumstances are likely to worsen. Act swiftly and smartly. Financial relief is just around the corner.

CHAPTER 5
Get the Hell Out of Debt

One of the biggest favours you and your partner can do for your relationship is to get out of debt fast and furious. Having debt feels like a ball and chain around your ankle, making it difficult to move forward with your life. It simply holds you back from achieving your full potential as a couple. Plus, debt causes mega money fights.

How you manage debt is a *huge* demonstration of your ability to manage your personal finances and overcome obstacles.

The fact is that most Canadians have some form of debt. Access to credit cards, loans, mortgages, and store cards has become easier and more prevalent than in previous generations. You can't walk through an airport or shopping mall anymore without being approached to sign up for a credit card or deferred-payment plan. Just before the Christmas holidays in 2015, I walked into the Bay on their Black Friday sale day to do my Christmas shopping. Everything was 30 percent off … and if you signed up for their credit card you got an additional 15 percent off. Because I'm a sucker for a great deal, I did it. I was shocked by how easy it was. They had me fill out an application form, then they swiped my primary credit card, and I was instantly approved for a $6,000 credit limit. The whole process took three minutes. I signed up because of the huge discount I received. But I also had the money in my bank account to pay the bill. That's where most people get into trouble — they overzealously apply for credit and don't have the money to pay off the bill.

Our generation has grown up regularly using debt to afford its increasingly expensive lifestyle — and *yes*, it *is* more expensive to live now than it was fifty years ago. Plus, younger generations are forking out significant money for university and college education. Between my two rounds of university, I spent over $110,000. That's the equivalent of a house in a small town!

Since the 1990s, Canadians have been on a borrowing binge. In 2015, for every dollar of disposable income, each household owed $1.63, whereas in 1990, that number was $0.85. As a result, household savings have dropped just below 4 percent, whereas in 1990 Canadians saved 12 percent. In raw numbers, Canadian households each owe approximately $27,000 in non-mortgage debt. Not surprisingly, the under-40 crowd is most heavily indebted and at the greatest risk of default.[1]

Do you have knots in your stomach as you're reading this? Don't fret. Besides avoiding debt completely in the first place, the second best strategy is to Crush It (see page 66 of this chapter).

DEBT 101

The money you originally borrow is called principal. To borrow money, you must pay a premium, which is called interest. Interest is the cost associated with borrowing money.

Far too often, I hear, "The total cost of borrowing doesn't really concern me, just the monthly payments do." This is nonsense. Of course a monthly payment seems reasonable; it's the total cost of borrowing (principal plus interest), broken up into so-called easy and affordable monthly payments. This is a much easier sell for salespeople than trying to move a product at the *real* full price. Low monthly payments can trick you into thinking you're getting a good deal when you're not. A monthly payment of $100 when you're being charged 20 percent interest is never a good deal! Take a good hard look at the real cost of borrowing, which is the interest rate you pay.

Interest is typically based on risk. If you're likely to default on your loan payment, you'll pay a lot more in interest than someone who's less likely to do so. The way creditors determine who is and is not a risky person to lend to is based on credit history. If you have a good history (that is,

---

1 "Infographic: Canada's Households Now Owe a Record $1.8 Trillion." *Globe and Mail*, May 8, 2015. www.theglobeandmail.com/globe-investor/personal-finance/household-finances/canadian-households-now-owe-a-record-18-trillion-and-more-debt-statistics/article24322565.

you haven't missed payments), you're a less risky candidate than someone with a bad history of repayment.

As mentioned previously, building good credit can be done by making payments on time, in full, and toward debts that are in your name.

GOOD VERSUS BAD DEBT

Who knew some debt could be good? Good debt is debt that helps you grow your asset base: things you own. A mortgage, investment loan, and a business loan (for business investment) fall into the category of good debt. A mortgage on a home that appreciates steadily over the long term, for example, is a tool that helps you grow your assets. I also like to include student loans in this category because edu-

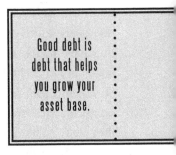

Good debt is debt that helps you grow your asset base.

cation is a huge asset that helps grow your income. Wondering about your car? *A car is not an asset.* The value of a standard vehicle doesn't appreciate in value over the long term; indeed, its value plummets the moment you drive it off the lot. Other than the very rare case — like a fancy antique Ferrari — 99.9 percent of vehicles won't appreciate in value, hence they aren't assets. Car *loans,* however, are bad debts. Good debts tend to cost the consumer a great deal less in interest when compared to bad debts.

Bad debt doesn't help grow your asset base. Credit card debt, car loans, and other types of consumer loans are typically used to purchase depreciating assets. The payments you're making on your living room furniture fall into the bad debt category as well. Interest rates on bad debts tend to be high.

Bad debt results when you use credit to purchase a consumer item that doesn't grow in value. For example, if you buy a big-screen TV and pay for it with a store credit card, not only will that TV be worth next to nothing in two years, but you'll be paying the original ticket price *plus* the high interest on the card.

Bad debt has zero return on investment other than it might increase your personal happiness factor until the next latest-and-greatest product hits the market. Your consumer-spending quick fix is both expensive and worthless in the long run.

Going forward, the best strategy for you and your debt, besides avoiding it completely, is to borrow to invest in assets and avoid debts that don't help increase your net worth.

THE UGLY TRUTH ABOUT CREDIT CARDS

Steven and Jean-François are 32 and 38 years old, respectively. Together they make $150,000 per year. They enjoy golfing and going to sports games; they share a nice car and take off to Vegas a few times each year. For years, they have managed their $10,000 credit card balance by making monthly payments of $500, but then racking it up again and never paying it off. Steven and Jean-François feel justified in their spending because they get points on their credit card toward flights that they use for their trips, but they are frustrated because they can never seem to pay the balance down.

Credit cards are a convenient way to pay for things you want whether you can or cannot afford to do so. If you don't carry a balance, and if you charge an item to your card, you've got 30 days to pay it off without paying interest on the purchase. If you can't pay off the balance, your credit card company will charge interest, typically 17 to 22 percent, on your purchase. Remarkably, many store credit cards charge even higher interest rates — some in the range of 28 or 29 percent. And heaven help you if you carry a balance and continue to put charges onto your card; your grace period on new purchases is less than three weeks.

Credit card debt accumulates quickly and can be difficult to pay off for three reasons: first, high interest rates; second, credit card companies set minimum payments at between 2 to 6 percent of the outstanding balance (or $10, whichever is higher), which barely covers the interest charges on the card; and third, interest is calculated and charged *daily*, not monthly (but you only see one interest charge per month on your credit card bill). You also need to keep in mind that as you pay off your credit card balance, your minimum payment will decline — a declining credit card balance means that the required minimum payment is constantly recalculated because the minimum payment is typically set as a percentage of the balance and so it decreases. This can extend the amount of time it will take to pay off the balance, as some consumers will simply make only the minimum payment.

This is why owing money on a credit card is financially lethal, forcing us into a situation where we are continually paying for the past rather than investing in the future!

Back to Steven and Jean-François for a moment. Their credit card company charges 19.5 percent in interest. By making payments of $500 each month toward their $10,000 balance, it will take them 25 months to pay it off ... and that's if they stop spending. But if Stephen and Jean-François make only the minimum payment, it will take them approximately 169 months to pay off the total if the minimum payment is 4 percent of the balance — that's over 14 freakin' years!

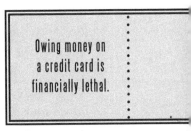

Owing money on a credit card is financially lethal.

Now, suppose you purchase a few new outfits from your favourite store at a cost of $1,000 using your regular credit card, which charges you 19.5 percent interest. The minimum payment on the bill that you receive will likely be about 4 percent of your total balance, meaning $40. If you make only that minimum payment, you'll barely be covering the interest! Almost none of your payment will go toward the principal amount owing. If, however, you simply commit to paying $40 each month, despite the declining balance, it would take you about 33 months to pay off that initial $1,000, versus 74 months if you were to pay only the minimum.

So, before you whip out that card, think about whether or not you can afford to pay it off within 30 days. If it's going to take you months to clear your balance, you might want to hold off on your purchase.

Guilty of racking up your credit card? Try these tips:

- Have only one or two cards. *No one* needs more than one or two credit cards. Self-made millionaires have only one or two cards and they don't carry a balance. Go into your wallet, remove all but one or two cards, and cut up the rest. If what's left is maxed out, so are you.
- Phone your credit card company or bank and ask them to remove you from their mailing or telephone-solicitation lists. This puts you on the "do not call" or "opt-out" list.

- Hide your cards. Bury them in the backyard, give them to someone you trust for safekeeping, or lock them up. Out of sight, out of mind.
- Reduce the credit limits on your cards as you pay them down. So, if your limit is $10,000, reduce it to $5,000 and then $2,500 once you've paid it down that much. Having a high credit limit actually occupies the remaining credit you have available, which can impact mortgage and other loan applications.
- Once your credit card balances are reduced or eliminated, call your credit card company and set up automatic balance payments each month. With this arrangement, your credit card company will debit your bank account each month for the full balance owing on your card. It's kind of like having a charge card where you must pay the card off in full each month. If, for example, you charge $300 on the card one month, your bank account will be debited by $300 and the payment applied to your card.

CRUSH IT

Think for a moment about what your life would be like if you were debt-free. Doesn't it feel awesome just thinking about it? Of course it does. And it's totally possible to get there by following the Crush It debt-reduction system.

Step 1: Get Specific

The first step to getting out of debt is to get specific about what you owe, to whom, and how you got there. You have to face the truth of your situation to create a successful plan to tackle it.

Start by listing your debts. To do this, dig up your monthly debt statements: credit cards, store cards, vehicle loans, personal loans, mortgages, and promissory notes. Using some type of tracking tool, like a spreadsheet, write down the outstanding balance, interest rate, and required monthly payment for each debt. Document everything —every hundred, every thousand, and every dollar you casually borrowed from friends and family too.

I recommend arranging the debts from left to right by decreasing interest rate. By doing this, you'll be able to see exactly what you owe, to whom, and how much (in terms of interest) it costs to carry a given outstanding debt.

Meet Taizelle and Gurinder. They owe:

- $2,500 on their Visa at 19.5 percent
- $3,000 on their MasterCard at 10.5 percent
- $11,000 on their consolidation loan at 9 percent
- $25,000 on their car loan at 6 percent
- $300,000 on their mortgage at 4.5 percent

TAIZELLE AND GURINDER'S DEBT

	Visa	MasterCard	Consolidation loan	Car loan	Mortgage	Total
Balance	$2,500	$3,000	$11,000	$25,000	$300,000	$341,500
Interest rate	19.5%	10.5%	9.0%	6.0%	4.5%	
Monthly payment	$75	$90	$330	$750	$1,700	$2,945

Now that your debts are staring you and your partner straight in the face, you need to have a discussion about how got you here and what you can do to avoid this situation in the future. Avoid finger pointing and arguments. Stick to the facts and talk about making tangible changes to your spending behaviours. To help with this conversation, try asking the following questions of yourself and each other:

- How does debt make me feel?
- How does my spending make you feel?
- What triggers our overspending?
- Do we have regrets about our purchases?
- How has debt affected our lives?
- Do we/I need professional credit counselling? (Hint — if you're not keeping up with payments, the answer to this question is YES.)

This kind of conversation is difficult but important. If you get stuck, take a break and return to it another day.

Step 2: Negotiate and Consolidate

Not surprisingly, wealthy people tend to be grinders — meaning they negotiate aggressively for the best prices and rates — and you should be too. The next step of Crush It is to call your lenders and start negotiating the interest rates on all your debts. Why? The lower the interest rate, the faster you'll pay off your debts. A good discussion can lead to thousands of dollars in savings. Why pay extra when negotiating can be as quick as a 10-minute chat with each lender?

Let's say, for example, that you owe $8,000 on your credit card. If you make minimum fixed payments of $240 per month at 19 percent interest, it'll take approximately 48 months to pay off that initial balance. If, however, you negotiate your rate down to 10 percent, it'll take 40 months *and* save you about $1,500 in interest charges.

If you're wondering what your debts are costing you, check out the Financial Consumer Agency of Canada (fcac-acfc.gc.ca) for cost-of-borrowing calculators on car loans, credit cards, mortgages, and other personal loans. Another great website that has calculators is the Innovations, Science and Economics Development Canada site, ic.gc.ca (select "Get Out of Debt" from the "Just for Consumers" drop-down menu). The American site bankrate.com also has a number of useful calculators. By using these tools to try out different interest-rate scenarios, you can see the impact a better rate will have on the time it takes to pay back a debt and how much you'll save.

Here's what you need for your interest-rate negotiation:

1. Research the current rates so that you know what's currently being offered in the marketplace and you have a realistic idea of what to aim for in your negotiation. For mortgages and credit card rates, I like to check ratehub.ca. For the Canadian government's overnight rate, check out bankofcanada.ca.
2. Call your lender, speak to a representative, and ask for a better rate. Remember, if you don't ask, you don't get!

This is where you present a competitive offer. Generally speaking, I'd recommend targeting at least a 5 to 10 percent decrease on credit card interest rates and a 2 to 5 percent decrease on all other consumer loans. Mortgages can be more difficult to negotiate (refinance), as they are typically locked in for longer terms, but still investigate whether it's a worthwhile option for you.

3. If you're not getting anywhere with the representative, speak to a manager. Managers tend to have more authority to negotiate and work with you. Ask for a lower rate and explain why, from a customer-service perspective, the bank should work with you.

4. If that still doesn't work, prepare to take your business elsewhere — somewhere they'll give you a credit if you switch over your business. Most credit grantors will try to work with you to keep your business, especially if you're a good client.

Sometimes lenders will try to saddle you with fees and penalties for re-negotiating. Just be aware that these extra costs are negotiable too. Whatever you do, *ensure that the benefits of renegotiation outweigh the costs* (especially with the renegotiation of a mortgage). This is when cost-of-borrowing calculators can really help. You can evaluate the impact of saving money on interest compared to fees and penalties your lender might charge.

Sometimes negotiating doesn't work. Depending on your interest rates, you may want to consider a consolidation loan or debt transfer to a line of credit. A consolidation loan places all your debts into one loan at a lower interest rate, allowing you to make one monthly payment instead of multiple payments. A line of credit is similar to a credit card; you receive an available credit limit and you must cover the interest each month, but the principal payment tends to be flexible. These options can provide much lower interest rates than a credit card or personal loan. When they are secured (meaning that you've posted collateral) against an asset such as your house, the rates are even lower. The most common secured line of credit is a home equity line of credit. When they are unsecured (no collateral posted), their interest rates are higher. So, be aware that you can use collateral to lower your rate.

If you don't have collateral, you can still work with your lender to get the lowest possible rate, and if you have great credit, emphasize that.

Both the line of credit and consolidation loan are offered at most financial institutions. The key with a consolidation loan or transfer of balance to a line of credit is discipline — do everything in your power to avoid getting into additional debt. You don't want to spend four years paying off your loan and then have to get another one because you haven't been responsible with your money throughout that time.

There are two other things to be cautious of when negotiating the interest rates on your debt. First, if you're dealing with a credit card company, ensure that your new interest rate is a permanent one. You don't want to have a temporary rate that will increase after a certain period of time (typically six months). Credit card companies often refer to these as "introductory" or "limited-time-only" rates. Second, do not charge additional purchases on your credit card while you still have a balance. Your interest charges will increase dramatically because the high rate will be applied to an even higher balance. If necessary, cut up your credit cards so that you're not tempted to spend.

Back to Taizelle and Gurinder. They agreed to split the task of negotiating with their creditors and are successful in renegotiating their Visa and consolidation loan. Their debt chart has now changed and looks as follows:

	Visa	MasterCard	Consolidation loan	Car loan	Mortgage	Total
Balance	$2,500	$3,000	$11,000	$25,000	$300,000	$341,500
Interest rate	12.0%	10.5%	7.0%	6.0%	4.5%	
Monthly payment	$75	$90	$330	$750	$1,700	$2,945

Step 3: Pay a Little Extra on the Highest-Interest Debt

Tackle the highest-interest debt first because it costs you the most. Many people focus on the amount owing rather than the interest rate. This is a common mistake. It may be more gratifying to pay off the smaller debts first, but if you're paying more interest on certain debts, they are, in fact, costing you more than necessary. Concentrate your efforts on the highest-interest debt first. Once that is eliminated, shift your attention to the next highest-interest debt.

In Gurinder and Taizelle's case, their Visa card costs them the most, followed by their MasterCard. Therefore, they should focus on paying a little extra on the Visa first.

I know your budget is probably really tight, but even just a few extra dollars can make a big difference over a long period of time.

Try cutting back a few coffees or lunches each week. Maybe change the brand of certain groceries you buy to one that's more affordable. You might be able to scrounge up $10 or $20 in a week that can be directed toward your debt. The Frugal Fundamentals in chapter 4 (see page 56) introduce some practical tips to saving.

Because these extra dollars are not a part of your minimum payment, they go straight onto the principal amount and not to interest charges, meaning that you'll pay off the debt that much sooner.

Take an extreme case, where you're carrying a $30,000 balance on your credit card at 19.5 percent. On that amount, your minimum monthly payment would be at least $600 or 2 percent of your balance owing (depending on your interest rate, the card, and the credit agreement). In the initial stages of your payments, approximately $500 would be applied to interest charges and only $100 to the principal debt. As time passes, and if you carry on paying $600 each month, more of your payment goes toward the principal and less toward interest expenses. At this rate, you'd be looking at almost nine years' worth of payments before you were debt-free!

With this in mind, let's say you've decided to pay a little extra on your credit card debt — $800 each month versus $600 on that $30,000 balance. By the end of the first 12-month period, you'll have paid $9,600 on your credit card, yet your remaining balance would still be approximately $26,000 — kind of deflating! But if you continue these $800 monthly payments, it will take five years to pay off that original balance, which sure beats nine years.

Paying a little extra can be easier at certain times of the month versus others and that's because expenses can pile up at different times. Pay a little extra when it makes sense for your cash flow. For example, because Gurinder and Taizelle's mortgage payment comes out of their account on the first of the month, they're financially strapped on that date. But when the 15th of the month rolls around and they receive another set of pay-cheques, that's when they can afford to pay a little extra — approximately $50 — on their Visa balance.

Just as a side note, paying a little extra — even $5 to $20 a week — can't be at the expense of your regular payments on your other debts. If you don't pay those, they will become delinquent, meaning that your creditors will report you to the credit bureaus, and that can seriously mess up your credit score.

And as a side, side note, the key to success with paying a little extra is to pay approximately two weeks after your first payment and then continue making these extra payments biweekly. Because of the way interest rates are calculated (especially on credit cards), you can significantly reduce the amount of time it takes to pay off your debt. This is because you are tackling the principal amount more frequently.

Remember that as you focus on making these extra payments on the highest-interest debt, you're also making progress toward reducing your other debts.

Step 4: One Down, On to the Next

Once you've paid off your highest-interest debt, you'll move on to the next-highest-interest debt. The great thing about this is that you'll have the previous regular payment plus you'll already be in the habit of paying a little extra — so you can plough all of that money into your second most expensive debt. In Gurinder and Taizelle's case, their regular payment on their MasterCard is $90 per month, but they will now have an additional $75 from what they were paying regularly on the Visa plus the extra $50 they found in their budget — bringing their monthly payment on the MasterCard to $215. Once the MasterCard is paid off, they can move on to their consolidation loan and following that, their car loan. All the while, the amount they can afford to pay increases with the elimination of the previous debt — it's kind of like an avalanche.

I recommend that you track your progress, or balances, on a spreadsheet every month. This way, you can watch the balances evaporate. There is nothing more motivating than crushing your debt. Again, the Crush It system assumes you don't accumulate further debts. Sometimes you will have to use your credit card for an emergency, and if you do, pay it off immediately, then get back to the Crush It system.

There is nothing more motivating than crushing your debt.

Without including their mortgage, Gurinder and Taizelle will become debt-free within three years using the Crush It system. If they decide not to use the system and simply make the regular payments at the original interest rate, it would take four years and cost them an unnecessary $1,300 in extra interest charges. Imagine Gurinder and Taizelle's delight at getting to debt-free a whole year sooner than expected.

Step 5: Don't Accumulate More

Seems logical, doesn't it? But the vast majority of people who become debt-free rack up more debt in the process of paying off existing debt. Don't let this be you. It will completely erode your net-worth progress and likely depress your spirits.

The Crush It system works! It's really that simple. The theory doesn't change, no matter how much you owe. Focus on the interest rate, pay a little extra on the highest-interest debt, pay it off, then transfer your energy and money to the next-highest-interest debt.

When Gurinder and Taizelle are consumer-debt free, they will have $1,295 per month in free cash flow (including the money from their regular payments plus the $50 extra from their budget). That's a lot of money that they can put toward saving more for retirement or reducing their mortgage (see page 94 for tips on how to burn your mortgage).

HAVE DEBT AND SAVINGS?

What if Gurinder and Taizell both have RRSPs, some savings, and all this debt? If their savings aren't earmarked for retirement or an emergency fund, they can apply them to their most expensive bad debt.

Think of it another way. If you have $2,000 kicking around in a savings account within your TFSA, that isn't being used for retirement savings or an emergency fund, and it's earning 2 percent annually, it's better to apply that $2,000 to your credit card balance, which is costing you 18 percent.

When You're in Too Deep

Sometimes debt can spiral way of control, in which case you may need credit counselling. Credit counselling is for people who need help creating a plan to manage extreme levels of debt, are headed for bankruptcy, or can't keep up with payments. In this situation, you work closely with a credit counsellor who will assess your total debt situation, help you develop a repayment plan, and negotiate interest rates with your creditors if necessary. Credit counsellors also offer solid advice to help you avoid bankruptcy.

If you're getting into debt faster than you can climb out, contact a nationally recognized not-for-profit credit counselling agency such as consolidatedcredit.ca, creditcounsellingcanada.ca, or creditcanada.com. Be wary of credit counselling agencies that are not endorsed by the government. Although they may claim to "fix" your credit by having negative reports removed from your file (in exchange for payment), that's impossible. Unless there is a reporting error on your credit file, your credit score can't be manipulated. There's only *one* legitimate way to fix bad credit: work with your creditors to repay debts and allow time to pass. Bankruptcy and foreclosure hurt both you and your credit provider, so try to work with your creditors to arrive at a potential solution. They'll be more willing to negotiate with you if you're serious about paying up, and they'll avoid writing off a bad loan.

Know Your Score

These days, having credit can be more of a liability than in the past. Consumers have to watch out for identity theft and corporate reporting errors. To mitigate any risks, get a copy of your credit report to cross-reference your list of outstanding debts to that of the credit bureau, and ensure that your credit file is up to date and accurate. If it's not, you need to deal with the credit bureau and lenders to get it corrected.

To ensure that your credit file has accurate information, check it every one to two years. You can order your report online or by mail.

If you have a question or inquiry, send a written request (with official receipts and paperwork that help validate your side of the issue) to the credit bureau so it can investigate.

If an error is discovered in your file, the credit bureau must correct it. If an error is corrected, the credit bureau will send copies of the updated file to the credit grantors if you request that. If a credit application is refused, the credit bureau isn't responsible for the decision; the credit grantor makes the decision based on its lending policies. If you're declined, you'll be directed to contact the credit bureau to review the information that contributed to the decision.

Visit the Equifax Canada (equifax.ca) or TransUnion Canada (transunion.ca) websites to learn more about getting your credit report.

STOP THE ADDICTION

Overspending can be like an addiction to drugs or alcohol. Buying the next greatest television or new car provides an instant hit of satisfaction that quickly disappears, leaving you wanting more. To succeed in overcoming debt, as with most challenges in life, you must come to terms with the behaviours that got you into debt in the first place. Lying to yourself about having spending or debt problems means your situation won't change. If you've got a debt problem, come to terms with it, take control, and learn to change your behaviour. Do it together, as a team!

CHAPTER 6
Own the Walls You Live In

Buying a home is a massive decision and a house is probably the largest purchase you'll make in your entire life. So, it is no wonder that so many couples feel faint when signing on the dotted line of their first offer to purchase agreement. I was the same.

I purchased my first home, in Calgary, Alberta, right out of university at the age of 21 when house prices houses were still reasonable. I literally had sweat droplets on my forehead as I handed the realtor my deposit cheque for $10,000 — an amount that had taken me four and a half years to save.

> The benefits of home ownership can far outweigh the costs.

I moved in a few months later and quickly got into the groove of making my biweekly mortgage payment. That house was a huge financial stretch for me. But, thankfully, for the first four years I had housemates who helped to cover the cost of utilities and prop up my cash flow. I also received small but regular annual raises and had a small business, which allowed me to make a few extra mortgage payments every year plus take an affordable vacation.

Seven years later, after ploughing loads of equity into my home and having benefitted from the strong Alberta economy, I sold my place for double what I paid. I was then able to purchase a much better home in a better location with a small mortgage.

The benefits of home ownership can far outweigh the costs. First, you're growing your assets. Rather than paying rent (in other words, putting your money toward your landlord's mortgage), you are investing money in an asset that builds equity. Equity is the difference between the value of the home and value of the mortgage. So, as you pay down your mortgage, you increase the equity you have in the property. It's similar to having money in an investment.

Second, real estate has proven to be a very sound long-term investment. Through the ups and downs of the market, Canadian real estate has returned approximately 5.5 percent since 1980. Regardless of what's happening right now in the real estate market, keep a long-term perspective in mind when you plan on purchasing property.

I do, however, believe that the days of making a quick buck in real estate are coming to an end and we are returning to normal growth rates. This is simply due to the fact that housing affordability has gone way down in the past decade as the cost of homes in major centres has soared, making homeownership an unattainable dream for so many young couples.

Another benefit of owning a home is that it forces you to budget, save, and develop healthy financial habits. Paying a mortgage commands financial responsibility. You're on the hook for coming up with your mortgage payment and if you don't, the bank will seize your home. Paying a mortgage is essentially paying yourself first. Yes, you pay the bank back for lending you mortgage funds, but you're also putting money toward the equity in the home and *you* — not the bank — own that equity.

It's true that most self-made millionaires own rather than rent. However, it can make more sense to rent when the cost of homes is through the roof and would stretch the budget of homeowners beyond what they can reasonably afford. We've seen this first-hand in cities like Toronto and Vancouver over the past decade: young couples leaping into real-estate bidding wars that push them into borrowing hundreds of thousands of dollars more than they can truly afford in their monthly budget. Low interest rates over the past decade have allowed for couples to borrow significantly more money — sometimes hundreds of thousands more — than if rates were only two or three percentage points higher.

When I first moved to Toronto in 2015, I worked with a couple that had a combined income of $125,000. They somehow qualified for a mortgage of $750,000 and promptly went out and bid $900,000 — a whooping $150,000 over the list price — on a home in a great neighbourhood. Lo and behold, they won the deal and moved into their 1,300 square foot downtown gem four weeks later. After the champagne and moving trucks were gone, this poor couple was left with a fantastically large mortgage and literally no money left in their bank account for things such as a new furnace or roof repair. They actually had to sell their car in order to afford much-needed electrical work for their home. Not surprisingly, raging arguments about money started breaking out between them. This scenario — where a couple can barely afford anything but the cost of the home — is classic home poverty. No vacations, cars, furniture, or meals out.

In this instance the couple would have been better off renting for another few years to build up further savings and grow their incomes. Sure, they would have missed out on the ever-appreciating Toronto real estate market, but holding off would have better prepared them for the true costs of home ownership.

Don't let this be you.

RENTING VERSUS BUYING

Feel like you're missing out by renting? You're not. In certain circumstances, such as an overheated housing market, or if your income or credit score is too low, it makes more sense to rent rather than buy a home. For example, you might not be able to afford the total costs of home ownership, which go well beyond the mortgage payment. You'll be on the hook for utility bills, taxes, maintenance, and perhaps condo fees. Sometimes these extra expenses can be as much or even more than your mortgage payment! If you're a disciplined renter, you can save more money for retirement or a down payment by renting — hopefully investing the money into a quality asset that will grow in value. When you're ready to buy, you'll have those savings to put toward your home.

In the long run, however, home ownership usually makes senses for three reasons:

- Now or in the future, market rents will exceed your total home-ownership costs of mortgage payment, property taxes, and maintenance costs.
- Down the road, you'll pay off the home and your mortgage payment will disappear. When this happens, your housing

costs are significantly reduced and you'll free up major cash. If you rent, however, you will continue paying rent as long as you live in that home.

- When you put a down payment on a house, it is only a portion of the home's value (for example, 10 percent). But you still get to use 100 percent of the home and you experience 100 percent of the long-term appreciation of its value. So you actually get to "leverage" for an asset that's expected to grow.

THINK YOU'RE READY TO BUY?

Long before you start searching for property online or with an agent, you need to figure out what you can afford. This exercise can be very sobering; nevertheless, it's important to know your facts so that your ownership expectations are realistic. Ultimately, you'll need to determine if owning a home is going to put you into financial jeopardy (*serious* home poverty, to the point where you can't manage your other financial commitments). The only way to figure this out is to run "as-if" budget scenarios that includes the costs of:

- A mortgage
- Condo fees (if applicable)
- Heating/cooling
- Electricity and water
- Property taxes
- Home and life insurance
- Building up an emergency fund over a three- to five-year period (you'll need at least 5 percent of the home's value)

I would be remiss ignoring the fact that if you're thinking of buying a home you may also be weighing the pros and cons of having children, if you don't already have them. It's simply the same life stage. So, if this is you, your as-if budget scenario must also include parental leave and the exorbitant costs of child care in most provinces.

There are three other important financial considerations if you're going to buy: saving a down payment, affordability, and contingency planning.

Saving for a down payment: It's always a smart idea to have at least 10 percent of the value of the home, though you can secure a mortgage with 5 percent (but I don't recommend this). If you want to purchase a place for $500,000, you'll require at least $50,000. If you have less than 20 percent down, you'll have to pay fees to Genworth Canada or the Canadian Mortgage and Housing Corporation (CMHC) for what's known as an insured mortgage. An insured mortgage protects lenders in the event that a borrower stops making payments toward their mortgage. It is mandatory for mortgages where the down payment is between 5 and 20 percent. The lower your down payment, the higher your mortgage insurance fee. That's because you're considered higher risk. In a few pages, we'll focus on techniques to build up your down payment quickly (see page 82). By the way, if this is your second property, you'll need a minimum of a 20-percent down payment because you're an even higher risk to the bank.

Affordability: What you can afford to borrow is based on your income. There are three ways to determine this. First, go to the bank and have a personal banker tell you; second, check any of the big banks' websites and use their mortgage calculators; or third, tackle the calculation yourself using the lending thresholds described next.

Banks have specific lending thresholds for mortgages. Your gross debt service ratio is calculated by adding the following monthly or annual expenses:

- Mortgage payment
- Property taxes
- Heating costs
- Half of the condo fees (if applicable)

Together, these costs can't be more than 32 percent of your gross income (if you added the annual expenses, compare them to your annual income. If monthly, then compare to monthly income).

The second lending test banks use is called the total debt service ratio, which takes into account your other monthly debt obligations — basically the same list plus:

- Credit card payments
- Line of credit payments
- Vehicle loans
- Other debt obligations

When added to the total of the previous list, the value of both can't be more than 40 percent of your gross income.

No, you don't get to pick between these two measures. You're evaluated on both. The moral of this story is threefold. First, the more debt you have, the more it will erode what you can borrow. Second, the more money you make, the more you can borrow. Third, and probably the most important, is that the more expensive the home, the higher your ratios and financial risk to the bank.

Knowing what goes into calculating the debt service ratios is helpful because it clearly identifies the levers you can pull to improve them: your debts, your income, and your desired home price. In other words, the more you make and the less you owe, the more you can afford.

I'm a huge proponent of going to the bank and getting a pre-approval for your mortgage prior to hiring a realtor; in fact, most agents won't even take your business without your having done this. For a pre-approval, your personal banker will take you through the mortgage application process — addressing interest rates, mortgage structures, amortization periods, and so on — without executing any contracts. They will clearly identify your housing affordability using the ratios we just walked through, plus, they'll take into account your credit score. That's right, your credit score speaks to your level of financial responsibility and the banks are pretty square when it comes to this. If you don't fit into their perfect "good little borrower" sandbox, you're hooped. No mortgage for you. You'll have to hit up the secondary lending market, which can cost much more to borrow from.

Generally speaking, if you can't get pre-approved for a mortgage, you'll either have to pay cash for the entire cost of the home or have someone co-sign a mortgage with you. Otherwise, you'll have to keep saving up, reducing your debts, and improving your credit score while you wait until you can get approved for a mortgage. This can take months or years depending on the condition of your finances.

Many couples are shocked to learn how much money they can borrow. But just because you can afford to purchase a $700,000 home doesn't mean you should. Think about what impact home ownership will have on the rest of your finances (saving, investing, vacationing, education, children) now and in the future.

> Think about what impact home ownership will have on the rest of your finances now and in the future.

Contingency fund: Bad things can happen to good people. I read a self-help book about this years ago and discovered that sometimes honest people get screwed over extra badly because others take advantage of them, they don't ask questions, and/or they are simply ignorant of the facts of a situation. This applies to home buying. Shit happens to a home and it can knock you off budget. Remarkably, however, most home "emergencies" can be detected well in advance if you have an independent home inspector and a hard-ass lawyer working for you — people who are honest, even if it means they'll break your heart and sink the deal.

But seriously, you need to know what you're up against when you purchase a home so that you can plan in advance. I'm talking about leaky roofs, furnace replacement, special assessments for condos, faulty water tanks, fences, cracked foundations, and electrical or plumbing overhauls. These things can bury you financially. If you have a contingency fund, you're way more likely to weather the financial storm caused by unforeseen expenses and may even come out ahead.

As previously mentioned, this fund should be approximately 5 percent of the value of the home, and it will take time to build up. So, if buying a property leaves you no meat on the bone —that is, you have no money left over in your budget each month to put toward a contingency fund — you need to step back and reduce your purchase-price expectations.

SAVING FOR A DOWN PAYMENT

A down payment is the portion of money you put toward the purchase of a home that acts as the bank's security when it lends you the remaining amount in the form of a mortgage.

As mentioned, in Canada, you'll need at least 20 percent of the value of the home to have an uninsured mortgage. For the majority of younger buyers, this amount is too steep, so through the CMHC or Genworth Canada, a high-ratio (insured) mortgage is constructed through your lender (interest rates may be higher on insured mortgages). Typically, you can borrow up to 95 percent of the value of your home, meaning you'll have to come up with the remaining 5 percent; but again I don't recommend that. It's better for your financial well-being to put down at least 10 percent.

So how do you go about saving a down payment? Well, saving in a chequing account and hiding cash in a safety deposit box are counter-productive; these savings earn little or no interest and are too easy to dip into. Instead, you can use automation and low-risk savings tools such as a high-interest savings account, a GIC, or a money market mutual fund, all of which pay interest or generate a return but also protect your capital. Automation is sim-ple — on payday, have the amount of money you think you should save taken from your bank account and transferred into your chosen savings plan. Here's a helpful hint: don't link your down payment account to your debit card. You'll be tempted to spend that money.

> Another approach to save for a down payment is to stack GICs.

Let's pretend that you plan to make a down payment toward a condo in five years. The condo will likely cost $400,000 and you'd like to save 10 percent ($40,000) to put toward it. The easiest approach is to break the down payment up into smaller chunks — so, $40,000 divided into 60 months, or five years. This means saving approximately $667 every month. If you get a bonus, by chance, or receive a nice commission on a sale you worked on, great! You can put it toward your down payment and get to your goal a little faster. What will also help speed you along is the interest you'll earn on your funds. Sure, it won't be remarkably high, but something is better than nothing.

Another approach to save for a down payment is to stack GICs. GICs are guaranteed investments that pay a small, but respectable, interest rate on your money. You'll never lose a dime, but you'll never double your money either … unless you're willing to wait 40 years. With GICs you invest your money for a set period of time and receive a set interest rate.

A stacked GIC involves investing in GICs regularly through automatic contributions and coordinating the maturity dates of the GICs. So, you can stack your GICs until you are set to buy a home, all the while protecting capital and earning interest, and have them mature when you're ready.

Let's go back to the previous example where you and your love want to save $40,000 for your down payment. You can contribute monthly to a GIC that will mature in five years, when you expect to purchase your home. Or you can contribute in lump sums, on a yearly basis, when you both earn bonuses, get your tax returns, or get paid for extra contract or freelance work.

You choose the latter approach and scrounge up $8,000 per year to make a lump-sum contribution to your down payment fund.

In your first year of saving, you tuck away $8,000 at 2.6 percent to mature five years from now. The second year, you tuck away $8,000 at 2.25 percent to mature in four years. The third year, you tuck away $8,000 at 2 percent to mature in three years. At the beginning of the fourth year, you tuck away $8,000 at 1.5 percent and have it mature in two years. In your last year, you tuck away $8,000 at 1 percent set to mature in one year. Each of these GICs will mature at the same time, having earned interest (and having been protected) throughout the five years. Here's how it looks:

STACKED-GIC SAVING STRATEGY

	Year 1	Year 2	Year 3	Year 4	Year 5	Total Savings
Amount invested	$8,000	$8,000	$8,000	$8,000	$8,000	
Interest rate	2.60%	2.25%	2.00%	1.50%	1.00%	
Years invested	5	4	3	2	1	
Value at maturity	$9,096	$8,745	$8,490	$8,242	$8,080	$42,652

As you can see, you earn approximately $2,650 in interest in this example. That money could go toward your legal fees when closing the property, paint for your new kitchen, or land transfer taxes. To avoid paying tax on the interest you earn, save your down payment in a TFSA or your RRSP (if using the RRSP Home Buyers' Plan). You can withdraw the money at any time without paying tax, and the extra-awesome part about it is that you get your contribution room back! That means you can re-contribute the amount of money you take out over the coming years. We'll discuss the benefits of the RRSP Home Buyers' Plan on page 86.

I like the stacked-GIC approach because it earns a variety of rates of interest. If rates go up, you have the opportunity to take advantage of them in the year you purchase your GIC. Unfortunately, the same applies if rates go down. But, more important, your money is safe and earning a respectable level of interest.

Whether it's a down payment or another big-ticket item like building up your contingency fund, you can save money through monthly or lump-sum contributions. The key to success is simply automation and not linking that account to your debit card.

Down Payment Gifts

Another way to secure a down payment is through a gift from a family member. This might feel like a cop-out but it's not. Sometimes family would actually prefer to give you money when you really need it rather than leaving your inheritance until much later. I worked with a couple a few years ago, Jose and Maria, who were in this exact position. With three young children and a modest income, it would have taken them over a decade to save the $30,000 they would need for a 10 percent down payment on a home valued at $300,000.

Together we approached their parents and asked for the gift of a down payment. It turned out they were elated to help. Jose and Maria had been struggling financially for years and this was a meaningful opportunity for their parents to help give them, and their children, a leg up. The parents felt great putting their money to good use, while the couple benefitted from not paying rent any longer, and instead, starting to build equity.

I personally had a similar experience when my grandmother helped me pay some of my tuition for my undergraduate degree. She got to watch her investment in me grow into my eventual career. That put a huge smile on her face and to this day, she still talks about it.

If you think this could be a good option for you, start the dialogue with your family.

The RRSP Home Buyers' Plan

The RRSP Home Buyers' Plan allows you to borrow up to $25,000 tax-free from your RRSP to put toward your down payment, with certain restrictions — namely, that you are a first-time homebuyer. If you buy a home with a spouse or common-law partner, you can each withdraw up to $25,000 for a total of $50,000. You'll then have 15 years to repay the funds back into your RRSP.

The reason I like the Home Buyers' Plan is that as you are building your savings up within your RRSP, you get to defer your taxes on the contribution you make. When you withdraw the money for the Home Buyers' Plan it's with pre-tax dollars, and for most Canadians that's the equivalent of saving 26 percent extra. Normally you pay taxes on money withdrawn from your RRSP when you retire. But you don't have to pay tax on the money if you use it for the Home Buyers' Plan.

The tax deferral that comes with contributing to an RRSP shows up in the form of reduced taxes on an annual basis, and in many cases, a tax refund. Let's look at a quick example of someone who earns $30,000.

RRSP TAX DEFERRAL

	$0 RRSP contribution	$3,000 RRSP contribution
Taxable income	$30,000	$30,000
Combined federal and provincial tax bill	$7,800	$7,020
Deferred tax	$0	$780

Making a $3,000 contribution to an RRSP results in deferring $780 in taxes. That money can simply be reinvested straight back into the RRSP, further building up savings for a down payment. In the opposite scenario, not investing $3,000 into an RRSP results in zero tax savings. There are very few investment opportunities I can introduce to you that will save you 26 percent on your tax bill, effectively increasing your take-home income. Yes — I know you will pay the taxes later in life. But, similar to the gifting principle introduced in the previous section, don't you want your money working for today, rather than waiting it out until retirement?

On the flip side, there are a few reasons that the Home Buyers' Plan might not work well for you. First, when you take money out of your RRSP, you lose the power of compounded interest and reinvested returns on those funds. Money grows exponentially over time, and when you reduce the money in your RRSP account, you earn less interest and sacrifice potential returns on what typically performs better than real estate — the stock and mutual or index fund markets (which have returned between 9 to 12 percent annually over the past 50 years).

Second, you can't make a repayment into your RRSP in the same year you take money out of it. You can start repayments only in the second year following the year of withdrawal.

Third, when you repay those borrowed funds each year, you don't get any tax write-offs on those repayments because they aren't considered RRSP contributions; it's not new money.

As long as you're aware of both the benefits and drawbacks, the choice is up to you. In my opinion, however, the benefits of using the Home Buyers' Plan (if you can) outweighs the costs in most situations.

Ready to Shop?

Now that you've saved up your down payment, you're ready to shop! Consider whether you want to use a real estate agent. Agents work on commission and sometimes their interests differ from yours. But there are many benefits to working with a good agent: they're knowledgeable about the real estate market (where, when, and how to buy) and how to conduct a successful real estate transaction. Often they have access to real estate information such as price comparisons or future community development plans, and they have access to better market information than you might have. If a house goes up for sale, they might be notified of the listing before it is posted for the public to view.

My realtor, for example, also just happens to be one of my best friends. She knows that I love a good deal and so when she comes across a great listing, such as an estate sale or a foreclosure, she calls me. The property may not be for my personal use, but it might fit well as an investment property. Having full days of family, friends, fitness, and work, I don't have time to scour the market to look for good deals like this, but she does. And those real estate investment opportunities add value to my net worth.

Before signing on with just one person, interview a few agents and phone their past clients for references. You'll want to work with someone who's competent, experienced, has a proven track record of integrity and high standards, knows how to negotiate, and understands finances well.

To find an agent, ask your friends and family for referrals. Next, check out local advertisements. Tour the areas in which you'd like to live and look at the for-sale signs on some of the houses that catch your interest. The real estate agent's name, phone number, and website are listed there.

If you choose not to work with an agent, you'll end up having to do all the research yourself. You'll have to research the areas in which you want to buy, learn the price points of homes, set up your own appointments to view homes, and educate yourself on how to conduct a real estate transaction. You'll also need to arrange for a home inspection and, if the inspector finds something seriously wrong, you'll have to deal with the legalities of backing out of the sale if you choose to do so. If you're willing to learn about successful real estate transactions, great! If not, doing it yourself can be a risky and costly endeavour. Carefully consider the time and risks involved if you don't use an agent. Unless you have a significant amount of time on your hands, it's going to be hard to manage the entire home-buying process successfully — especially if it's your first time buying.

The big reason people don't use realtors is to try to save money on the purchase price. Here's how: a seller's agent collects a fee for their services (which the seller pays — the fee is embedded in the purchase price of the home) and the fee must be split with the buyer's realtor. It's a fee based on the purchase price. The higher the selling price of the home, the more money both realtors are paid. Thus, a buyer's realtor isn't financially incentivized to get the lowest price and neither is the seller's realtor.

Take note here that if you're selling a home while in the process of buying a new one, and are using a realtor, you'll pay a hefty fee for the sale, plus your realtor will also make money on your purchase. The going realtor fees in Canada are anywhere from 5 to 7 percent.

Here's an example of how seller's and buyer's agents split their service fee: if a home sells for $300,000 and the total commission is 5 percent, that is a $15,000 realtor fee paid by the seller and split equally between the agents — so, $7,500 each. If that same home sells for $1,100,000, the realtor fee is $55,000 and when split equally, each realtor makes an extra $20,000, for a total of $27,500 each.

This example illustrates that both realtors are financially incentivized to sell you a home for as much money as possible rather than help you pay the lowest price.

So again, if you're going to work with a realtor and pay them a stack of cash, make sure you're getting good value from them. Back to my realtor for another moment. In 2012 she helped me sell my first house and purchase another one. After scouring the market, she discovered an estate sale that no one wanted

> If you're going to work with a realtor and pay them a stack of cash, make sure you're getting good value.

to touch because it hadn't been maintained well and, let's face it, death can make buyers uncomfortable. My realtor and I negotiated hard with the estate and bought the property for $100,000 under market value. I did a quick and semi-inexpensive cosmetic renovation ($25,000) and moved in, making $75,000 (on-paper) in the course of three months. My awesome realtor earned every penny of her commission because she helped me build my net worth through this transaction. That's why I continue to use her.

A good realtor who wants a long-term relationship with you will always act in your best interest. But when their personal interests outweigh your interests, you can run into trouble. Don't hire someone who is lazy or has a bad reputation.

To set both yourself and your realtor up for success, make sure you're clear about what type of home and price range you're looking for before shopping. A good agent will stick to your guidelines and provide information and ideas that are within your boundaries.

Wish List

Whether this is your first, second, third, or tenth property (for investment or personal use), prepare a wish list. Write down your preferences for each of these elements:

- Price range
- Resale or new
- Desired neighbourhood or community (urban, suburban, or rural)
- Proximity to
  - Schools
  - Shopping
  - Places of worship
  - Workplace
  - Public transit
  - Emergency services
  - Major roads
- Type of home (townhouse, attached, detached, apartment, duplex, low-rise, or high-rise)
- Freehold or condominium
- Age of home
- Number of bedrooms
- Number of bathrooms
- Fireplace
- Gas or electric stove
- Exterior (brick, vinyl siding, wood, or other)
- Foundation (wood, concrete, aluminum, or other)
- Age of roof
- Age of furnace
- Age of hot water tank
- Age of electrical and plumbing systems
- Deck
- Patio
- Parking (driveway, street, or garage)
- Yard
- Fixer-upper or renovated
- Security system

- Air conditioning
- View
- Quiet/busy location
- Traffic patterns
- Other important features

SELECTING A MORTGAGE THAT WORKS FOR YOU

Once you've signed off on your offer to purchase agreement, it's time to pick a mortgage that works for you.

There are several elements to consider in a mortgage. The amortization period is how long it will take to pay off the total mortgage, which typically ranges from 5 to 25 years. If you have a down payment larger than 20 percent, you can sometimes secure a 30-year mortgage. Remember that the longer you take to pay off your mortgage, the lower the payments, but you'll pay much more in accumulated interest.

The next item is the term of the mortgage, which is how long your mortgage contract will last. It typically ranges from 6 months to 5 or 10 years. When the term expires, you can renegotiate certain terms of the mortgage loan, transfer your loan to another institution, pay it off, or renew it for another term. Another way to think of the term is that you're taking the total amortization period and breaking it down into smaller chunks. So, if you have a 25-year amortization, you could break it down into five terms, for example.

Every term has an interest rate associated with it. The interest on a mortgage is the premium you pay to the bank for lending you money, as you would with any loan. The difference with a mortgage is that you have a choice when it comes to interest rates: they can be fixed or variable. A fixed interest rate means that the bank can't change the rate for the full term. A variable rate fluctuates with the prime rate, and is typically lower than the current posted fixed rate. But the rate can fluctuate. If the rates increase, less of your payment gets applied to the principal. If the rates decrease, more of your payment gets applied to the principal. Fixed rates are less risky than variable rates, but they'll cost you a bit more. Variable-rate mortgages are also harder to qualify for and there are more stipulations in the fine print because of the risk.

Carefully select the type of interest rate based on your risk tolerance. If you're risk-averse and will lose sleep with a variable-interest mortgage, don't sign up for one. Pay the extra interest for more comfort. On the other hand, if you don't mind fluctuations, sign up for a variable mortgage and save some money relative to the going fixed rate, but be prepared to pay more interest if the rates increase.

It's important to consider the interest associated with the term. The longer you stretch the term, generally the more interest you'll pay. So, a five-year fixed mortgage will have a higher rate than a three-year fixed mortgage. But who knows where rates will go. By the end of your five-year term, the going rate could be much higher and you will have saved money on interest through your previous term. Banks charge this extra interest to mitigate the risk of rate increases (they can't change yours because you'll have locked in at a low rate). On the other hand, the longer you lock in at a fixed rate, the less flexibility you have; if rates fall, you're locked into paying the higher rate unless you pay money to renegotiate, or "break," your mortgage.

A short term means your mortgage comes up for renewal more often. You'll also have to weather the ups and downs of interest rates more frequently. This can be a good or bad thing depending on where rates go. If rates go up, you'll end up having to pay more once you renew. If they go down, you'll end up paying less.

Here are my suggestions. If you're a brand-new homeowner, on a tight budget, and slightly risk-averse, consider a fixed rate for a term of four to five years. Your payments won't change and you'll be able to manage your budget for years to come. You'll also avoid the stress associated with interest-rate fluctuations. Just be aware that this option costs you money to feel safe.

If you handle risk well, can afford a higher payment if rates increase in the future, and have a bit more home-ownership experience, check out a shorter-term variable-rate mortgage. You'll save money on mortgage costs, meaning that more of your payment will go toward principal rather than interest. But remember that if rates increase, you'll have to pay more in interest.

There are also two hybrid mortgages. The first is called a rate-capped mortgage, which takes advantage of a variable rate. If the rate increases to a certain level, the mortgage locks in for the remainder of the term (thus capping the rate). Be aware that you do pay a premium for this type of structure. The second is a convertible mortgage, which means the terms can be converted to new terms (hopefully more favourable ones) after a certain period of time.

From an Economics 101 perspective, it makes sense to lock in for a longer-term fixed-rate mortgage when overall interest rates are super-low. These rates could eventually increase and cost you more if you were on a shorter-term variable-rate mortgage. On the other hand, it makes sense to sign up for a shorter-term mortgage when rates are high because interest rates will hopefully start declining, saving you money by not locking you into a high rate.

Whatever your risk tolerance and mortgage preference, always keep a long-term perspective. Interest rates and home values can rise and fall quickly, and their fast movements shouldn't trigger a knee-jerk reaction on your end. Stay focused on your long-term goals.

The last thing to consider when selecting a mortgage is whether you want it to be open or closed. An open mortgage costs more because it's super-flexible. You can, at any time throughout the term, pay any portion of the mortgage loan off without penalty. This option can be valuable if you expect your income to increase or if you expect to come into additional money that could be used to pay off or pay down the mortgage. You can negotiate almost any term of an open mortgage at almost any time. For example, if you don't want a variable mortgage but still want to tinker around with falling interest rates, you could get a fixed mortgage that's open. That way, your rate is fixed, but if overall interest rates fall, you can renegotiate and lock into a lower rate. Keep in mind, though, that open mortgages can cost a lot more than closed ones.

A closed mortgage means you are committed to the terms and conditions of the mortgage until your term is up. A closed mortgage costs less because it guarantees the lender a steady stream of payments from you. If you wanted to make changes to the loan, you'd likely be stuck paying heavy penalty fees. On the bright side, closed mortgages have become quite competitive and now lenders offer additional prepayment options for these types of loans.

Finally, the interest rate can often be negotiated. Even one-half of a percentage point lower can save you thousands of dollars. Shop around for the most competitive rates and terms. Check out all the big bank websites as well as ratehub.ca. Keep in mind that sometimes your primary banking institution will provide the most competitive rates for you because you have other business with them.

BURN YOUR MORTGAGE

Imagine being mortgage-free sooner. Your cash flow would be greatly increased, allowing you to invest more and improve your overall lifestyle. Most mortgages allow you to pay extra on the principal balance without having to refinance or renegotiate the mortgage terms.

A double-up payment means simply that you pay up to double the regular monthly, biweekly, or semi-monthly payment. If your regular monthly payment is $1,500, you could pay up to $1,500 extra as a double-up payment each month.

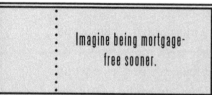

Imagine being mortgage-free sooner.

Most lenders also allow between 10 to 20 percent of the original value of the mortgage as an annual lump-sum payment in addition to your regular payment schedule. If your original mortgage was $150,000 and your lender allows up to a 10 percent annual lump-sum payment, this translates into a $15,000 lump-sum payment you can make every year.

If your lender will allow it, set up accelerated weekly or biweekly payments rather than monthly payments. Accelerated payments are slightly higher than regular payments, and the increased frequency translates into extra payments each year.

While setting up accelerated weekly or biweekly payments, round up to nearest $100. If your biweekly payment is $470, round it to $500.

Accelerated payments can be easier for homeowners on a tight budget with fixed cash flow when compared to double-up or lump-sum payments. The extra amount you pay is small and is tacked on to the regular payment. This allows you to build a fixed amount into your budget. But if a homeowner benefits from infrequent extra money like bonuses or tax refunds, double-up or lump-sum payments could be easier. Some lenders allow you to increase your regular payments at certain points throughout the term of the mortgage.

Wondering where you can scrounge up extra money to pay off your mortgage faster? Any time you receive extra money through a tax refund, birthday present, or performance bonus, put it on your mortgage. Cut back on restaurant dining, theatre tickets, and shoe shopping. Trade in your expensive car for one that's more affordable. Even small cost reductions can save hundreds. Sell unused furniture and electronics. Bundle and renegotiate utility and cellular bills. Take on extra hours at work or turn a hobby into extra income.

Remember, this isn't all guesswork. By making a quick call to your mortgage lender, you can determine the specific prepayment options available with your mortgage and set yourself well on the path to paying off your home faster.

HAVING TROUBLE GETTING APPROVED?

There are many reasons that mortgages don't get approved, including bad credit, low income, and debt. Here are some ideas of what you can do if you're getting declined due to the following reasons:

Low income: If the bank tells you that you can't afford a particular mortgage amount because of your income, it's for good reason: you won't be able to afford the payments. To overcome this, try the following:

- Lower your mortgage expectations by shopping for a cheaper home.
- Start making more money.
- Put more money down. A bigger down payment means a smaller mortgage.
- Get someone to co-sign the loan with you. If you know someone who's willing to back your loan, you can have him or her sign with you on the mortgage as assurance to the bank that at least someone has the ability to make the payments. This can be a very helpful option for entrepreneurs with variable income levels.

Too much debt: This is part of getting your financial house in order. Multiple credit cards, a line of credit, a vehicle loan, and other consumer debt will contribute to the bank's decision to decline a mortgage loan. A large chunk of what the bank believes you can afford is based on the credit that is *available* to you. For instance, if person A has a MasterCard with a balance and a credit limit of $5,000, and person B has three credit cards with no balance and credit limits totalling $15,000, person A poses less risk than person B because person B has the *potential* to utilize $15,000 of credit, whereas person A has access to only $5,000 of credit. Here's what you should consider doing if you've got too much available credit:

- Slowly begin to consolidate consumer debt to reduce your overall available credit. Cancel unused credit cards (keep the one with the best and longest credit history), transfer balances, and ask the lender to reduce the credit limit or both.
- Focus on paying down consumer loan balances quickly, especially if they're getting in the way of owning a home. Go back to chapter 5, Get the Hell Out of Debt, for speedy debt-reduction strategies. The faster you get rid of your consumer debt, the more available income you'll have to allocate toward a home.

Credit: Before you enter into the application process, review your credit report. To ensure that your credit file has accurate information, check on it every one to two years. If you've been late with payments, have missed payments, have not repaid a loan, or have declared bankruptcy, you're going to have a tough credit rating to overcome. If you have a history of financial irresponsibility in the eyes of the bank, lenders may decline your mortgage application. Here's what you can do:

- Be responsible and wait it out. Nothing speaks louder than your actions. If you really want to clean up your credit score, you'll have to prove you're responsible with money. Make your payments on time, don't miss payments, and don't ignore your debts. If you're struggling to keep up, see a credit counsellor who can help you negotiate new terms with your lenders.

INCREASE YOUR HOME'S VALUE

Does your new place need a pick-me-up? Perhaps the appliances, paint, or lighting aren't suited to your tastes. Or maybe you plan to live there for a short time and want to upgrade only the bare essentials. Whatever your situation, there are plenty of frugal home improvements that will add value to your new digs.

Before you take a sledgehammer to your dilapidated 50-year-old garage, step back and make a list of the repairs or replacements you want to make to your home. It helps to consult your home inspection report because it lists what needs attention and how critical each item is.

Next, prioritize the items. Hint — furnace repairs are essential in Canada and should take precedence over installing a custom-built Ping-Pong table.

Then investigate the cost of each item.

If you're like most new homeowners, your list of improvements will add up to be something quite substantial. Stick to a budget and work through your list over the course of a few years.

I recommend kicking-off your improvements with 50 to 100 hours of thorough cleaning and basic handyman/woman fixes: cabinets, drapes, floors, walls, closets, knobs, handles, changing light bulbs, hanging doors, tightening loose screws, and fixing leaky taps. In the past, I've watched YouTube videos that explain how to fix home basics like sinks and tubs that are slow to drain. These actions are free, can save thousands of dollars, and will allow you to better determine whether you can repair rather than replace certain elements of the home.

Move to the highest impact items next. Have your furnace, water heater, and air conditioning unit inspected, repaired, and cleaned. Upgrade appliances and faucets, refinish cabinets, re-grout tiles, and replace knobs and toilet seats. Reduce clutter by setting up well-designed storage spaces. Update light fixtures and carpets, or refinish worn-out hardwood. Hire an electrician and plumber to fix any electrical or plumbing issues. Paint your walls and furnish your home with appealing items.

Many affordable home improvements can be completed by you, which saves money. When purchasing supplies, furniture, or appliances, check for gently used items on eBay, Craigslist, or Kijiji. I once bought a new stove from a builder's model show home, still in its original packaging, for $60.

It's easy to add value to your home through sweat equity and affordable upgrades.

Sometimes home renovations require the services of a contractor. Be sure to:

- Make a list of exactly what you want done.
- Set a clear budget.
- Ask for recommendations from friends and neighbours.
- Get written estimates from at least three contractors and don't accept any over the phone (verbal quotes are quickly forgotten).
- Observe the quality of questions the contractor asks carefully (gives an indication of their level of experience).
- Consider dealing with a local company, making it easier to check references, enforce a warranty, or have follow-up work done.
- Ask for at least three references and go view the work the contractor did.
- Cross-reference the name and company of your contractor against charges or convictions through the Consumer Protection Act, Google Reviews, and "Consumer Beware" lists for your area.

If you're satisfied, review the contractor's contract with your lawyer, paying special attention to terms and conditions.

As you and your partner work through your home improvements, don't forget to check out available tax credits for your home renovations.

CHAPTER 7
Invest Like a Pro 1.0: Be Yourself

People avoid investing for a million different reasons — and most of them are completely bogus. Since the 1960s, excuses have included President John F. Kennedy's assassination, the Watergate scandal, Y2K, the bird flu pandemic, 9/11, and the terrorist attacks in Paris.

Researchers at BMO Bank of Montreal compared the "excuses people" with the "no-excuses people" and found that people who had invested $10,000 in the TSX Composite Index in 1960 and left their investment alone (that is, they didn't respond to the latest and greatest news) had investments worth more than $1 million over 50 years later. Meanwhile, the "excuses people" didn't earn a return because they'd continued to find reasons not to invest.

When you wait to invest, you lose time, which affects your exponential growth potential. If, for example, you start investing $150 a month at the age of 20 and earn a 9 percent annualized return on your portfolio, by the time you retire at 65, you'd have approximately $1 million in your portfolio. Not a bad sum of money considering you had to contribute only $81,000 of your own money. The rest was earned through the power of compounded interest and reinvested returns.

But if you wait to start investing until you're 40, using the same scenario, you'd have less than $200,000 in your portfolio. If you wanted to have that that same $1 million by retirement, you'd have to save $900 per month and earn a 9 percent annualized return on the portfolio. In total, you'd invest $270,000 of your own money to achieve the same result. That's $750 more each month than if you'd simply started saving at age 20.

The longer you wait to invest, the more you lose out. So start now with as much as you can afford to invest. You'll make it much easier on yourself later in life.

You're probably wondering where the heck you'd earn a 9 percent rate of return. Well, since the 1970s, the stock market (measured by the S&P 500) has increased nearly 200 percent, and on an annual basis that has meant a return of between 9 and 12 percent throughout the long term. Meanwhile, savings-account returns have been much lower, ranging from 1.5 to 3 percent — not even keeping up with inflation. Let's assume that you invested $1,000 in 1970 in a diversified stock market portfolio. If you gained a 200 percent average long-term return, your original $1,000 would be worth nearly $200,000 today!

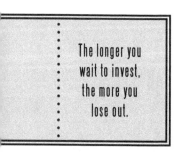

The longer you wait to invest, the more you lose out.

North American equity markets (the stock market) have typically performed better than any other type of single investment in the long run. If you take the time to understand how the markets work, and what investments are best for you, you can certainly do well over time.

Before we get into investing strategies you and your love can follow, I want to make one thing very clear: educated investing in the stock market, or any market for that matter, is not the same as gambling; however, investing *based on little to no information* is. So don't invest your life savings in the stock of your best friend's software company without knowing how to evaluate the investment first.

I absolutely love the Abraham Lincoln quote "Give me six hours to cut down a tree and I'll spend the first four sharpening the axe." Investing is similar. Take the time to sharpen your investing knowledge before placing your trade order, hiring a broker, or quitting your day job to become a day trader (which I don't recommend even to the most seasoned investors).

Investing wisely will help you and your partner achieve financial freedom — whatever that means to you. Having enough money for retirement? To buy a business? To travel the world? To change careers? We each have our own definition of financial freedom, but ultimately it means having the ability and choice to do what you want to do. And luckily, a little bit of knowledge coupled with some first-hand experience is all you need to invest successfully.

INVESTMENT BASICS

Investments are not the same thing as an investment plan. Investments are stocks, bonds, mutual funds, index funds, and exchange-traded funds, and also derivatives and stock options. Each investment has a certain risk associated with it, and the risk should match your risk personality.

Investment plans such as RRSPs, TFSAs, and pensions, on the other hand, are like holding tanks filled with investments. In many cases, investment plans have been created in conjunction with the government or an employer, or both, to help Canadians save more through the provision of tax benefits. In other cases, non-registered investment plans provide limited tax incentives. That's why you should maximize tax-advantaged plans prior to investing in a non-registered plan. Why the heck wouldn't you want to save money on taxes?

> Educated investing in the stock market is not the same as gambling.

Investments can be broken into two categories: lending and owning. Lending investments work like this: you lend your money to an institution such as a bank, corporation, or government through investments like a GIC or a bond, and the institution promises to pay your money back with interest within a certain time frame. In many cases, your principal and/or interest rate is protected in some capacity. In other cases, lending investments provide a steady stream of income; hence, they're also known as fixed-income investments. The added protection can make these investments more secure than ownership/equity investments. The trade-off for extra safety is less potential return. Fixed-income investments tend to suit the profile of a more conservative or balanced investor, and we'll get to what that all means in a moment (see page 106).

Ownership or equity investments work like this: you buy a share or unit of a company or fund through an investment such as a mutual fund or stock, and you earn returns through appreciation (the increased value of the unit or share, called capital gains, which are incurred only when you sell). You can also make money on your investments through dividends. A dividend is a payment you receive for holding a stock — it's a reward for the risk you've taken on. So, for example, you may receive a dividend of $2 for a share that is worth $100. Mature companies tend to pay higher dividends than those companies focused on rapid growth. There's more risk associated with ownership investments because there's no guaranteed return and no protection of the principal amount of money you invest. Despite the extra risk, there's greater potential to earn more money than in lending investments, which means ownership investments often suit the profile of less-conservative, or higher-risk, investors.

In general, when you start investing, you can afford to have a higher risk tolerance because you have more time on your side to invest and generate a return. Higher-risk, aggressive investing works well when you have a long-term approach. But as you approach retirement, your time frame is reduced; at that point it's common to shift toward a more conservative investment approach focused on protecting your assets.

What's Your Number?

Investing success starts with understanding your risk tolerance. And, by the way, this is likely very different between partners. For once, you and your honey don't need to be aligned on risk. You simply need to invest in a way that honours your individual risk preferences. Studies show that those who honour their natural tendencies toward risk tend to generate a rate of return similar to the market (recall that historical returns have ranged between 9 and 12 percent), whereas investors who invest outside of their risk comfort zone barely keep up with the rate of inflation. That's because they hop around between investments rather than stay invested for the long term.

> Investing success starts with understanding your risk tolerance.

Thankfully, you and your partner can't share RRSPs, TFSAs, and pension accounts, so you can each invest according to your individual risk profiles.

Let's take Leigh and Carol, for example. They have different views on risk. Carol is super-conservative and doesn't believe in having any form of debt or in investing. She keeps her money in a high-interest savings account. Leigh is the opposite, owning leveraged investment properties and buying high-risk stocks. Instead of fighting about their differences, they have separate accounts for all their investments.

Would you go to work dressed in swimming trunks or a bikini? I doubt it. Unless you're a model for tanning lotion, you'd probably be sent home to change. Think of asset allocation, or the investments that make up your total investment portfolio, in a similar fashion: you don't want inappropriate investments in your portfolio because they won't meet your needs. When your investments match your risk tolerance, you're more likely to stay invested for the long term in quality assets.

Risk is a tricky thing: we strive to mitigate as much risk as possible while still trying to achieve the greatest reward. The risk-versus-reward relationship works like this: the greater the risk you take on, the greater the potential reward. The less risk you take on, the lower the potential reward. This relationship can be applied to investments within a portfolio: the riskier the investment, the greater the potential for a higher reward — and for serious losses.

Younger investors have more time to invest and they can generally afford to take on greater risks in the hopes of achieving greater returns. But as investors age, life's responsibilities creep in to their decision-making. There are more assets to protect, including things like your house, family, or retirement savings. Therefore, risk tolerance tends to decrease as investors age because there's more to protect.

Proper asset allocation also means that your portfolio is properly diversified, so all your eggs aren't in one basket. If you diversify, losing one egg won't be quite as devastating.

To allocate your investments properly, it's important to know your investment-personality type: conservative (1), moderate (2), balanced (3), growth-oriented (4), or aggressive (5). Sit down with your partner and take this fun investment-personality quiz designed to help you understand your financial situation, attitudes toward risk, investment timeline, and goals. Remember that you're probably going to have different responses, and that's okay!

INVESTMENT-PERSONALITY QUIZ

1. How old are you?

    a. 55 or older
    b. 45 to 54
    c. 35 to 44
    d. 25 to 34
    e. under 24

2. How many years away are you from retirement?

    a. 10 years or less
    b. 11 to 14 years
    c. 15 to 19 years
    d. 20 to 29 years
    e. 30 years or more

3. Which statement do you most agree with?

    a. I don't invest and I know diddly-squat about investments.
    b. I invest, but I know diddly-squat about the investments I've put my money into.
    c. I invest and I know basic investment information like the types of investments in my portfolio and where I bought them.
    d. I invest and I know what assets are in my portfolio and why I have them.
    e. I invest and I know what assets I own and why I have them, and I'm actively involved in managing my portfolio.

4. If the value of your portfolio plunges by 5 or 10 percent in one day, you feel

    a. Like vomiting.
    b. Nauseated, but you'll get over it.
    c. Neutral — you weren't paying attention.
    d. Aware, but you're fine.
    e. A-okay; it happens.

5. Are you willing to hold on to your investments even when their value plunges?

    a. No freakin' way!
    b. Probably not.
    c. Maybe, maybe not.
    d. Probably.
    e. Absolutely.

6. What statement do you most agree with when it comes to investing?

    a. I don't care what return I make, I just want to protect the money I have.
    b. I want the safest investments with the least risk possible.
    c. I want to make a modest return on my investments, so I'm willing to take some risks.
    d. I take time to evaluate my risks and I'll take a risk if the potential return seems worth it.
    e. I take higher risks because I know I'll get higher returns. I also know I can lose more if I'm wrong.

If the majority of your answers were "a," you're more conservative and would be ranked 1 out of 5.

If the majority of your answers were "b," you're fairly moderate and would be ranked 2 out of 5.

If the majority of your answers were "c," then you're more balanced and would be ranked 3 out of 5.

If the majority of your answers were "d," you're growth-oriented and would be ranked 4 out of 5.

If the majority of your answers were "e," then you're more aggressive and would be ranked 5 out of 5.

If you had a wide combination of answers, check out the following descriptions to see if any particular one seems to fit you better than another. Below each description is a graph that suggests the type of asset breakdown that might suit each investment personality type.

Most financial institutions offer clients a more comprehensive investment-personality questionnaire, which will help you fine-tune the types of investments that will suit your needs.

* * *

Conservative: A conservative investor is highly averse to risk and should select the least aggressive investments. Typically, conservative investors have a shorter investment time frame — for example, they're less than 10 years from retirement. Their primary focus is on asset protection and income generation. The majority of their assets fall into a conservative category, such as fixed-income investments (government and low-risk corporate bonds), cash, and some less-risky stocks that pay high dividends.

CONSERVATIVE

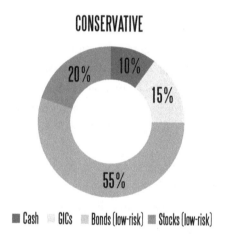

■ Cash   GICs   ■ Bonds (low-risk) ■ Stocks (low-risk)

Moderate: A moderate investor has a slightly longer investment time frame (15-plus years until retirement), but shorter than a balanced investor. A moderate investor still focuses on asset protection and wants their portfolio to grow modestly while generating a steady income. A moderate investor is comfortable with some risk, but is still considered risk-averse in the broad scheme of things. The moderate investor's portfolio tends to comprise fixed-income investments and some less-risky stocks that pay high dividends. Individuals who are somewhat risk-averse but want some measured growth fall into this category.

MODERATE

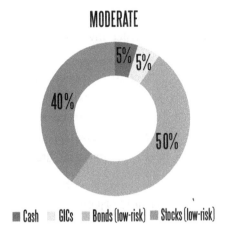

5% 5%

40%

50%

■ Cash   ▨ GICs   ▨ Bonds (low-risk)   ▨ Stocks (low-risk)

Balanced: A balanced investor is looking for long-term growth but still wants security and income. Their portfolio is balanced between medium- to low-risk equities that pay modest dividends and fixed-income investments. The balanced investor wants to grow their portfolio and is willing to take on calculated risk to achieve it. When in doubt, a balanced portfolio of half fixed-income investments and half equities is suitable for just about anyone.

BALANCED

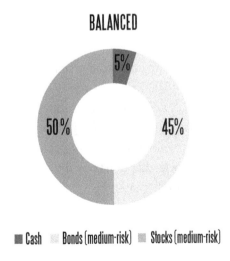

5%

50%

45%

■ Cash   ▨ Bonds (medium-risk)   ▨ Stocks (medium-risk)

Growth-Oriented: A growth-oriented investor wants significant long-term growth and takes greater risks for potentially higher rewards. This investor's portfolio primarily comprises growth-oriented stocks that will appreciate in value. Growth stocks tend to have higher risk, potentially higher returns, and lower dividends. A growth-oriented investor typically has a long time frame to invest their money and can handle market volatility. Again, younger investors generally fall into this category.

GROWTH-ORIENTED

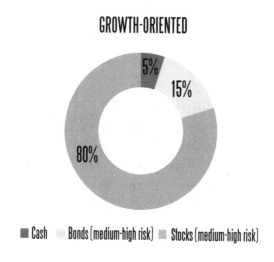

■ Cash   ▧ Bonds (medium-high risk)   ▨ Stocks (medium-high risk)

Aggressive: An aggressive investor wants significant long-term growth and is willing to take significant risk in order to achieve it. They have the potential to make the most and lose the most of any investment personality. This profile fits the individual who has a lot of time to invest and isn't concerned by short-term volatility. Their portfolio is made up primarily of aggressive high-risk stocks that don't pay dividends. More experienced investors generally fall into this category.

AGGRESSIVE

15%

85%

■ Bonds (high-risk)   ■ Stocks (high risk)

So, what do you think of your risk assessment? Is it what you expected? In the past I've had clients say to me that they would like to change their risk profile to be either more or less risky. But by now you know that you shouldn't, because you'll lose money on your investments. Honour your investment personality and you'll make money.

MARKET EXPOSURE

Your investments may be exposed to market risk. The financial markets are for securities. Securities are specific investments, such as stocks or bonds, that are traded on a market where buyers and sellers meet to buy and sell their specific securities. Investment experts tend to refer to two types of markets: debt (bonds) and equity (stocks).

The most commonly referred to and highly publicized market is the stock market. The stock market responds to different stimuli such as supply, demand, analysts' forecasts, and global political and financial turmoil. That's why when countries struggling with debt, such as the United States or Greece in recent years, and are at risk of defaulting on their debt payments, it affects other economies around

> Honour your investment personality and you'll make money.

the globe that are interlinked with theirs, and causes the Canadian stock market to swing up and down.

Markets are by nature cyclical. They go up and down, but overall they tend to increase in value as companies, and their associated securities — stocks and bonds — drive toward future growth and development. When a market gains in value, or "charges forward," it's called a bull market; when it declines, or "hibernates," it's called a bear market.

> It never hurts to look at the past, learn from it, and plan our investment strategies.

A bull market tends to last anywhere between 36 to 48 months, whereas a bear market typically lasts 10 to 12 months. According to Dundee, average bull market returns have historically been approximately 118 percent. Meanwhile, average losses in a bear market have been approximately 33 percent, demonstrating that in years past, market gains outweighed losses.

Though past performance is never a true predictor of future performance, history reveals, time and again, that staying invested for the long term pays off. History also gives us insight into how markets have reacted to major economic changes, which helps us to understand why and how the markets do what they do. So it never hurts to look at the past, learn from it, and plan our investment strategies for the future.

Depending on what you invest in, you'll be exposed to the ups and downs of the market to a greater or lesser degree. The less risky your investor profile, the less exposure to the market you'll want. The opposite is also true.

CHAPTER 8
Invest Like a Pro 2.0: Use the Right Plans

Tasha jokes with her co-workers that her retirement-savings plan is her weekly $10 lucky lotto ticket. For Tasha, investing isn't a top priority. She'd rather focus on planning her next vacation with her boyfriend. What Tasha doesn't realize is that if, instead of buying a $10 lotto ticket every week, she invested her money in a powerful tax-advantaged plan, her odds of being well prepared for retirement would be far greater than winning the lottery.

There are four powerful investment plans with associated tax advantages:

- Registered Retirement Savings Plan (RRSP)
- Employer pension plans
- Tax-Free Savings Account (TFSA)
- Registered Education Savings Plan (RESP)

REGISTERED RETIREMENT SAVINGS PLANS

If you're over 18 and employed or self-employed, you should contribute to an RRSP. In the majority of cases, the associated tax advantages make this the best tool for long-term retirement savings available to Canadians.

Annually, you're allowed to contribute 18 percent of your income up to an annual maximum, which is indexed for inflation each year, so check the

Canada Revenue Agency website (cra-arc.gc.ca) to assess your personal limit through the My Account feature of the website. If you contribute by more than $2,000 beyond your limit, you'll be penalized by Canada Revenue Agency (CRA) at a rate of 1 percent a month, so stick to the limit.

If you don't use the full amount of contribution room within your RRSP, you can carry forward the unused amount from prior years until December 31 of the year you turn 71 years old, which is the last day you can make a contribution to your RRSP . This is a fabulous feature of the RRSP because if you can't afford to maximize your contribution or you would prefer to defer the tax benefits of your RRSP until a year in which you make a greater income and could benefit more from the tax savings, you can contribute that amount the next year or the year after that or the year after that (you get the point), benefitting from the tax advantages then.

> The associated tax advantages make an RRSP the best tool for long-term retirement savings.

Contributions must be made by March 1 for a tax deduction for the previous year. For example, if your contribution limit for 2016 is $10,000, you'd have until March 1, 2017, to make your contributions for the 2016 tax year.

Funds within the RRSP grow tax-free until withdrawal, at which time you'll pay taxes. Many retirees will not make as much money as they did when they were working, so their tax rate can be lower. Your tax bracket is dependent upon post-retirement income streams such as pensions and income from investments. If, however, you take your money out pre-retirement, you'll get dinged with a withholding tax bill that can be between 10 and 30 percent. The withdrawal is considered taxable income. Also, you will not get your contribution room back.

Again, the major benefit of RRSPs is that you defer paying taxes on the money you invest, which is very useful when you're starting out in your career, purchasing your first home, growing your family, and travelling. Tax deferral allows you to maximize your savings opportunities today because less of your income is going to taxes.

Let's get to the stuff that you care about, though; for every $1 you put into your RRSP, you essentially receive $0.26 in taxes back (that's if your tax rate hovers around the Canadian average of 26 percent). It may be more or less depending on your tax rate. If, for example, you contribute $10,000, you'll save approximately $2,600 on taxes. This will show up in your annual tax filing and reduce the taxes you pay, resulting in a tax refund in many cases.

> Tax deferral allows you to maximize your savings opportunities today.

The next great thing about an RRSP is that you can select almost any type of investment to put in your RRSP — stocks, bonds, mutual funds, index funds, and exchange-traded funds.

How Can I Make the Most of My RRSP?

To get the most value from your RRSP, maximize your allowable yearly contributions, especially as your income and associated taxes grow. You get a greater tax deferral, plus you'll have a larger portfolio. Maxing out your RRSP may appear daunting, but the following strategy will make the process much easier without cramping your cash flow too much. I call it "Max Out the Easy Way."

1. **Start**: Set up regular RRSP payday contributions. For example, if you start contributing $50 every two weeks, you'll make 26 installments of $50, bringing your annual total contribution to $1,300.

2. **Take free money:** If your company has an RRSP savings program where they match a portion of your contribution, sign up. It's like getting a raise.

3. **Increase:** Increase your contributions each year. For example, turn that $50 biweekly contribution into a $100 biweekly contribution, bringing your annual total to $2,600. Increase it again the following year from $100 to $150 biweekly, bringing your total contribution to $3,900. If you're fortunate enough to get a salary increase, allocate part of that to your RRSP.

4. **Borrow to maximize:** After you're comfortable growing your contributions every year, consider an RRSP loan.

RRSP loans allow you to borrow money at a reasonable interest rate in order to maximize your contributions. If your RRSP limit is $10,000 for this year and you have already contributed $5,000, borrow the remaining $5,000 to maximize your contribution. An alternative to an RRSP loan is to borrow using a low-interest line of credit.

Why go into debt to invest in your RRSP? Two reasons: First, the more you contribute, the more you'll save on your taxes. This often results in a large tax return, which can then be used to pay down your loan. If you're not going to get a return, however, you should ensure that you can afford the monthly payments on the loan. Ideally, you'll want to pay the RRSP loan off within one year. Second, money grows exponentially. More money grows faster than less money through the power of compounded interest and reinvested returns. The more you save, the more you'll potentially earn. Back to our example from a moment ago: Let's say you're 30 and you decide not to borrow an extra $5,000 to maximize your RRSP. That $5,000 compounded at 6 percent for 25 years adds up to just over $21,000 before taxes when you're 55. Without the RRSP loan, you would miss out on tens of thousands of dollars in compounded interest and reinvested returns. And the $5,000 RRSP loan you could have gotten wouldn't have cost you anywhere near that amount in interest.

Keep in mind that the credit application for an RRSP loan is subject to the financial institution's lending criteria. Using borrowed money to finance the purchase of investments within your RRSP is riskier than using cash. Make sure you're comfortable with this risk. If you borrow to invest in your RRSP, negotiate for the best interest rate, read the fine print on the contract, ensure that you can make the monthly payments, and do it in a year when you are making more money, thus paying greater taxes. Also note that you cannot write-off the interest of your RRSP loan against your income taxes.

5. **Ease your way out of borrowing:** You'll use an RRSP loan yearly, but borrow less every year by contributing more of

your own cash to your RRSP. This will help wean you off RRSP debt over the course of a few years. I'd recommend using the RRSP loans for up to three years, at which point you should be maxing out your allowable limit yourself.

PENSION PLANS

According to Statistics Canada, just under half of Canadian employees utilize an employer-sponsored registered pension plan (RPP). This means that more than 50 percent of paid Canadian workers either don't have access to one or simply don't participate. Some companies have an opt-out clause that lets the employee choose whether to contribute to the RPP; other companies have mandatory participation. If you're fortunate enough to have access to a plan, don't opt out. With most company-sponsored pension plans, the employer kicks in free money or benefits. You can usually sign up within the first year of your employment.

> If you're fortunate enough to have access to a pension plan, don't opt out.

There are two main types of RPPs: defined contribution plans and defined benefit plans. The most commonly issued plan in Canada is the defined contribution plan. With this plan, you, and sometimes your employer, pay a predetermined amount of money into your pension. You get to choose from a pre-determined set of investments how the money is invested, and when you retire your pension is worth whatever the investments you selected previously are worth.

Because you make the investment choices for the plan, you are 100 percent responsible for the profits or losses associated with your decisions. So, if you make a bad investment choice from the available selection of investments, your employer isn't responsible for the outcome of that decision — likely a shortfall in your account.

Though this might sound risky, being in control of how your pension money is invested can be advantageous; especially in the case where your investments have grown significantly.

Most employers will match an employee's contribution up to a certain proportion. If you contribute 4 percent of your salary, your employer might match you 100 percent (in other words, another 4 percent). Or you might contribute 6 percent and your employer contributes 3 percent matching (50 percent of what you contribute). Whatever the specific matching program is, it makes sense to maximize your portion of the contributions into the plan for two reasons: you contribute with pre-tax dollars and you get free money from your employer.

Here's an example of how a defined contribution plan can work. Alan makes $40,000 a year as a junior sales representative for a pharmaceutical firm. He doesn't use his company's defined contribution pension plan. Instead, Alan invests 10 percent of his gross annual income, $4,000, with after-tax dollars, through his financial institution's mutual funds. Since the average Canadian pays approximately 26 percent of his or her income in tax and deductions, the tax and other deductions from Alan's gross pay amount to $10,400, which reduces his leftover income to $29,600. Out of that remaining $29,600, he invests $4,000, which means he has only $25,600 left to spend each year on things like rent, groceries, a cell phone, vacation, and other things. Investing $4,000 annually means he'll have to tuck away $333 per month.

Jake, on the other hand, works in the same department, makes $40,000 per year, but uses the company defined contribution plan. If Jake invests 10 percent of his gross annual income in pre-tax dollars ($4,000) into the company's defined contribution mutual funds, he ends up paying 26 percent taxes (and deductions) on $36,000, which amounts to $9,360. That's $1,040 less in tax than what Alan paid, leaving Jake with $26,640.

In both scenarios, Alan and Jake each invest $4,000 annually; however, Jake keeps $26,640, and Alan keeps $25,600. For Jake, that means he'll have an extra $1,040 per year, or $87 per month, to spend.

If that doesn't convince you to sign up for your company's plan, maybe this will. Let's say Jake and Alan's employer has committed to matching 50 percent of employees' contribution if they use the company's defined contribution plan. That means Jake saves $4,000 and his employer adds an additional $2,000 to his plan, for a total of $6,000 annually. In essence, this is like getting a $2,000 raise. Alan, who invests outside the defined contribution plan, will not reap the same benefits. If Alan and Jake both started their savings programs today and earned an 8 percent annual return over 25 years, Alan would have approximately $316,000 and Jake would have $473,000.

TWO APPROACHES TO SAVING FOR RETIREMENT

	Alan	Jake
Income	$40,000	$40,000
Investment in defined contribution plan	$0	$4,000
Taxable income	$40,000	$36,000
Taxes paid	$10,400	$9,360
Investment outside work in a non-registered investment plan*	$4,000	$0
Net income	$25,600	$26,640
Employer match	$0	$2,000
Investment value (8% annual return over 25 years)	$316,000	$473,000

*A non-registered investment plan that doesn't provide tax savings. Note that if Alan invested in an RRSP, he would benefit from nearly equivalent tax savings to Jake.

A minority of Canadians continue to enjoy a defined benefit plan. With this plan, you receive a defined or pre-set payout each month once retirement hits. The actual benefit received through a defined benefit plan is based on a formula that is applied to your income nearing the end of your employment, when you typically earn the most money. The details of the formula are located in the fine print of the plan. In certain cases, the defined benefit plan is 100 percent employer funded, while in others, funding it is the joint responsibility of both the employee and employer.

In the case of defined benefit plans, the employer shoulders all the risk associated with managing and funding the plan. Even

> Remember that more money grows faster than less money.

if the markets perform poorly, making the plan more costly to provide, the employer will still pay the same amount of pension promised to the employee.

From an employee's perspective, this plan is a worry-free solution to retirement planning. From an employer's perspective, this style of pension plan is expensive and has a great deal of risk associated with it. Since early in 2000, there has been a significant increase in employers underfunding defined benefit plans. This has been a large contributor to many employers opting for defined contribution plans, going forward.

The only thing pensioners have to worry about with the defined benefit plan is whether their employer goes bankrupt. But even if this happens, there is a great deal of legal protection for pension assets.

In either the defined contribution or defined benefit scenarios, if you leave your job, make arrangements to transfer your pension to a Locked-in Retirement Account (LIRA), established through a financial adviser or on your own through a self-directed investing account. Both the federal and provincial governments will not allow you to convert your pension into cash until you retire.

Similar to RRSPs, there are limits to the amount of money that can be invested in a defined contribution and defined benefit plan. These limits change every year so consult the Canada Revenue Agency registered plan limits (cra-arc.gc.ca/tx/rgstrd/papspapar-fefespfer/lmts-eng.html). When you and/or your employer contribute to a defined contribution (or a defined benefit) plan, your contribution does eat up a part of your RRSP contribution limit. Nevertheless, sign up and maximize the use of your company's plan. Remember that more money grows faster than less money — and take any opportunity to get free money! In 2016 for example, the Defined Contribution Plan limits are $26,010 whereas the RRSP limits are just over $25,370.

Self-Employed?

If you're self-employed or your employer doesn't offer a tax-advantaged retirement savings program, it's even more important for you to take the reins on investing for your retirement because you'll receive no help from anyone but yourself. To get started, you'll just need to open up your own tax-advantaged retirement investment plan through a professional invest-ment adviser at your bank. You can set this up very easily, either through your small business or personally. In both instances, the tax advantages are extremely powerful, so use them!

Popular plans that offer tax advantages are:

- Pooled Registered Pension Plan (PRPPs)
- Group RRSPs
- Individual RRSPs

In many cases, both the costs of setting up and contributing to retire-ment savings plans for self-employed people are tax-deductible expenses for a business.

TAX-FREE SAVINGS ACCOUNTS

The Tax-Free Savings Account (TFSA) allows Canadians 18 years of age and older to save and grow their money tax-free. There is a maximum amount you can contribute to the plan and it is indexed to inflation. For 2016, the limit is $5,500.

Though your contributions aren't eligible for a tax deduction, your earnings within the plan aren't taxed. Basically your money grows tax-free, even when it is withdrawn. With an RRSP, how-ever, you're taxed at your personal income tax rate when funds are withdrawn in retirement.

> The best way to utilize a TFSA is to maximize the allowable yearly contribution.

Similar to the other plans we've discussed, you can put a variety of investments within the TFSA, from GICs to stocks to mutual funds. Your contribution room is also carried forward indefinitely, so if you can't contribute one year, you can make up for it the next year.

When you withdraw the funds, which you can do without penalty at any time, you don't pay tax on capital gains, dividends, distributions, or interest earned. On the flip side of this, capital losses within the plan are not tax deductible and dividends aren't eligible for the dividend tax credit.

Another major benefit of the TFSA is that if you withdraw money, you can re-contribute that money one year after withdrawal. There is no time limit on re-contribution. This means that, in essence, you get your contribution room back. If you grew your TFSA to $30,000, you could withdraw it, not pay tax on its growth, and get your contribution room back for future contributions.

Unlike the RRSP and pension plans, the TFSA can be used for either short- or long-term saving, so a TFSA can be a great way to save for down payments, vacations, or weddings. However, if you invest for the long term, you'll reap the benefits of long-term growth and additional compounded interest and reinvested returns. Whatever your goals, the best way to utilize a TFSA is to maximize the allowable yearly contribution.

NON-REGISTERED INVESTMENT PLANS

Non-registered investment plans have fewer tax advantages. Returns generated within a non-registered plan do benefit from a dividend tax credit and a favourable capital gains tax rate (laws and regulations on taxes can change, so it's important that you research and review your current tax situation with a tax accountant). These plans are, in many cases, accounts for independent investments that don't fall within an RRSP, a pension plan, or TFSA. Non-registered plans come in very handy when you don't want to contribute to an RRSP or a TFSA, maybe because you've already maxed out your contribution limits.

Sometimes employers have independent non-registered savings programs such as a deferred profit-sharing plan or a share-purchase plan that employees can opt-in to in addition to their pension; if the employer contributes to it as well, it becomes a taxable benefit and you'll have to pay tax on the money contributed by your employer. Still, it's almost free money!

THE RRSP VERSUS THE TFSA VERSUS NON-REGISTERED PLANS

The primary difference between RRSPs, TFSAs, and non-registered investment plans is in the ways they're taxed. The following example illustrates this point.

If you want to invest $5,000 in an index fund that generates returns each year in each of the plans, and allow for all the returns to be reinvested and compounded at 8.5 percent annually for 25 years, you must contribute $6,750 pre-tax dollars to have $5,000 to invest in your TFSA and non-registered accounts. With an RRSP, you invest with pre-tax dollars and pay taxes later on. When you compare the total impact of taxes between the TFSA and RRSP, they are nearly the same. But, as you can see in the table below, the after-tax value of the non-registered account is much lower than the TFSA and RRSP. That is primarily because you'll be taxed yearly on those earnings.

TFSA VS. RRSP VS. NON-REGISTERED

	TFSA	RRSP	Non-Registered
Pre-tax contribution	$6,570	$5,000	$6,750
After-tax contribution	$5,000	$5,000	$5,000
Pre-tax value in 25 years	$38,400	$38,400	$38,400
After-tax value in 25 years	$38,400	$28,400	$25,100

*Assuming an investment income tax rate of approximately 28 percent and a personal income tax rate of 26 percent

As you can see, the RRSP allows you to get a head start on earning higher potential returns because the sum invested is pre-tax dollars. The TFSA requires after-tax dollars upfront. The non-registered plan ensures that you pay taxes throughout the course of the plan, which really eats into the amount of money you're able to earn and build. There are still benefits to investing in a non-registered plan, but the tax incentives in the TFSA and RRSP are generally more favourable.

Between the RRSP and TFSA, however, there are a few scenarios that might make one plan better for you than the other. If your income is high and you're paying more in taxes, the RRSP is more advantageous because the contribution limits are significantly higher than the TFSA's. This means you can defer a significantly larger portion of your taxes while building up more retirement savings. But if you have a lower income, you won't benefit nearly as much from the RRSP tax benefit, making the TFSA the better plan.

If you and your honey have a healthy household income, your first priority should be to maximize your RRSP contributions. Your Notice of Assessments will tell you how much contribution room you have available, or you can visit cra-arc.gc.ca/myaccount. Second, maximize your TFSA contributions. Third, contribute any additional savings into a non-registered plan.

If you can't max out your RRSP limit but still want to contribute to a TFSA, use a hybrid approach — I'd recommend a two-thirds RRSP and one-third TFSA split.

REGISTERED EDUCATION SAVINGS PLAN

For many parents, thinking of sending their children to post-secondary education causes a great deal of anxiety. Education is expensive. The projected cost of Canadian tuition for a four-year university degree in 2030 is approximately $115,000! No wonder talk of tuition scares so many parents! Planning ahead can reduce, and hopefully eliminate, the fear surrounding it.

If your child is under the age of 16, he or she qualifies for free government money through a Registered Education Savings Plan (RESP). An RESP is a fantastic tool that allows a parent, grandparent, friend, or legal guardian to save money for a child's post-secondary education. To set this up all you need is a social insurance number for the child and an appointment with your financial institution.

The Canadian government encourages saving by giving you free money toward your RESP through the Canadian Education Savings Grant (CESG) — 20 percent, up to $500 a year, of your annual contribution. Each child qualifies for a total lifetime CESG contribution of $7,200. If your child doesn't end up going to college or university, you can transfer the funds to another child within the family. If you have only one child or none of your children go to post-secondary, the RESP can be rolled into an RRSP, up to $50,000 tax-free, but the federal and provincial government grants and accumulated income and interest on the CESG portion must be repaid to the government. You can contribute into the RESP until your child is 21, but the government stops contributing their CESG portion when your child turns 17. Take advantage of the CESG while your child is young.

There are no annual contributions limits to RESPs but there is a lifetime limit of $50,000 per child. You can contribute the $50,000 all at once or you can contribute in smaller installments weekly, biweekly, monthly, or yearly. Note, though, that if you invest a lump sum of $50,000, you'll max out what you're allowed to contribute and you'll benefit from only $500 of the CESG grant. On the flip side, more money grows bigger and faster than less money. So, missing out on the total CESG is made up for through greater returns.

For most families, however, investing regular monthly contributions is more affordable than a large lump sum. The benefit of investing slowly over time is that you can take full advantage of the CESG.

You can set up an RESP as an individual plan with one named beneficiary so that each child gets his or her own plan, or you can set up a family plan for multiple children. Either way, the plans are pretty much identical. You may, however, save a bit of money in terms of account activity fees (administrative fees charged by your bank) with a family plan. Speak to your financial adviser about the plan details and what will work best for you.

When You Shouldn't Help Your Children

Though education is by far one of the best gifts you can give your child, one thing needs to be cleared up. You — the parent, guardian, or relative — should be contributing close to your maximum in RRSP contributions before saving for your child's education. Think of it in terms of an airplane pre-flight safety video instructing you to secure your own mask before securing your child's. The same thing goes for RESPs: contribute only after you've taken care of your own financial situation. You'll be in a much better position to help your children if you are on a solid financial foundation.

WHERE TO SET UP INVESTMENT PLANS

Most investment plans, except for a pension that is set up through work, can be established at any Canadian financial institution. Some of the leading institutions in Canada are:

- RBC Royal Bank (rbc.com)
- TD Bank Financial Group (td.com)
- CIBC (cibc.com)
- BMO Bank of Montreal (bmo.com)
- Scotiabank (scotiabank.com)
- HSBC (hsbc.ca)
- National Bank Financial (nbf.ca)
- Tangerine (tangerine.ca)

Choose an institution and adviser that you feel is right for you. Consider location, policy, customer service, and online and telephone access.

COUPLES INVESTING

There are certain limitations to a couple investing together. Yes, it's a nice thought to pool your money for more potential growth, but certain plans won't permit it. RRSPs, pension plans, and TFSAs are registered only in the name of the owner. That means you can't have joint ownership of these registered accounts. You can, however, contribute to a spousal RRSP, which allows you to shift income and associated taxes.

If you want to invest together — perhaps you are saving for a house — you can have joint ownership of a non-registered investment account. But I strongly recommend contributing to a joint non-registered plan only after your RRSP and TFSA are topped up, because these registered plans give a significant tax advantage and non-registered plans offer less of an advantage.

CHAPTER 9
Invest Like a Pro 3.0: Ready, Set, Go

By this point you and your partner should have a good idea of your respective investment personalities and the type of investment plans to build your portfolio within. Now it's time to unveil the types of investments available to you and strategies to make money with each.

ON THE MORE CONSERVATIVE SIDE

High-Interest Savings Accounts

A high-interest savings account is a useful tool for short-term savings. When you deposit your money in a savings account, you are, in essence, lending funds to the bank. The bank pays you interest (but not much) and then lends your funds at a much higher interest rate (more money for the bank). You can, of course, withdraw your funds at any time.

> A high-interest savings account is a useful tool for short-term savings.

Because of low interest rates, anywhere from 0 to 2 percent, savings accounts are not an effective tool for retirement savings. Savings accounts also tend to have high transaction fees. Ideally, this should encourage you to save and not withdraw frequently. But, overall, the account is very accessible (or liquid) and can tempt you to spend.

Your money is *really* safe when it's kept in a savings account and insured through the Canadian Deposit Insurance Corporation (CDIC).

A deposit of up to $100,000 is guaranteed by the Canadian government through CDIC for member institutions. A list of CDIC members can be found at cdic.ca.

Strategies with High-Interest Savings Accounts

Some online banks, like Tangerine and President's Choice Financial, offer higher rates and lower fees than bricks-and-mortar banks, due to their low overhead costs, and pass the savings onto you. Online banks can be accessed via telephone or the Internet.

If you're saving for a particular purpose, such as a vacation or an emergency fund, have a set amount of money automatically deposited into your high-interest savings account on payday. You can set this up at your local bank, over the phone, or online. I use my online banking to eTransfer money from my chequing to my savings account monthly. Sometimes I use this money to make lump-sum contributions to my investment accounts, other times it's put toward home repairs or a vacation.

GICs

A GIC is a low-risk lending investment similar to a savings account. You lend the bank money, it guarantees the principal and a set rate of return, and then it lends the money to other customers at a higher rate. Like a savings account, a GIC is a very safe investment type, but it typically pays a higher interest rate than a savings account; however, you lock up your money for a period of time ranging from 30 days to five years (and pay a penalty if you cash out early). Longer-term GICs tend to have higher interest rates because they tie your money up for a longer period of time, and the higher rate is a better incentive to the investor. Tying up funds in a GIC reduces the temptation to spend. You can purchase GICs at your financial institution for a lump-sum investment (minimums hover around $500) or in regular intervals (weekly, monthly, bi-weekly). Your GIC dollars are insured through the CDIC up to $100,000.

Strategies with GICs

Negotiate: Negotiate the rate of return on your GIC, especially if you have existing business with a bank. It's helpful to present a competitive offer from another institution offering a higher rate.

Beat low interest rates with GICs: To diversify risk and beat cycles of low interest rates, try a GIC-stacking strategy, like the one discussed in chapter 6 (see page 84). It works like this: buy GICs with staggered maturity dates and interest rates. For example, if you have $6,000 to invest, buy a $2,000 one-year GIC at 7 percent, a $2,000 two-year GIC at 2 percent, and a $2,000 three-year GIC at 2.5 percent. Each year, one GIC will mature and can be reinvested in a longer-term GIC, which tend to have higher interest rates. This strategy allows you to cash out of a short-term (low-rate) position and reinvest into a higher-returning GIC each year. Ideally, rates will rise while you're invested in the shorter-term GIC.

Bonds

A bond is also known as a fixed-income security or a debt instrument. When a company or government needs money, it can raise the required capital by issuing bonds. You loan your money to a company, like the Canadian Pacific Railway or Bell Canada, or to a government, like the Government of Canada, and, as with a GIC, you earn interest on it. The bond-issuing company or government will pay the bond interest at regular intervals throughout the period that you hold the bond. When a corporation or government issues a bond, the bond is a written legal promise that the bond issuer will repay a specified amount of money with interest after a specified amount of time. If the company or government happens to go bankrupt during that time, it is legally required to pay back anyone with a claim to the company's assets; bondholders fall into this category. No such promise exists with shareholders of stocks.

Most bond-issuing companies pay interest to the bondholder semi-annually for the amount of interest the bond gains throughout that period. This is often referred to as simple interest, which is interest earned on the principal but not compounded. Other types of bonds don't issue interest cheques at all. Instead, they wait until the bond matures. At that point, they pay back both the principal amount and the compounded interest. For investors with 20 plus years to retirement, compounded interest bonds tend to be more powerful than simple interest bonds, which don't reinvest the interest.

Because simple interest bonds pay interest regularly, they're a great way to generate fixed income. That's what make them attractive to retirees or conservative investors.

> Because simple interest bonds pay interest regularly, they're a great way to generate fixed income.

Bonds typically pay higher interest than GICs or savings accounts because they are slightly more risky. To make the most out of bond purchases, invest in and hold them for the full term so that you earn all of the interest payments and retain the bond's value.

Historically, bond prices have moved in the opposite direction of the stock market; bond prices respond inversely to interest rates. When interest rates drop, bond prices increase and vice versa. For that reason, bonds can provide good protection in the event of a recession. Sometimes they even perform well throughout a recession.

Other than daily postings of prices in newspaper business sections, there's very little available information on bonds compared to information on stocks. Bonds are traded over the counter between dealers (professional money managers) and not in an open market like the stock market, so it's difficult to get information on them. Securities regulators in Canada have expressed interest in improving the transparency within this market so that investors are better informed. In the interim, before you invest in a bond, specifically corporate and government bonds (not Canada Savings Bonds), you'll need to dig for information.

All corporate bonds are rated in terms of the credit quality of the issuing company's financial situation. In other words, is it at risk of defaulting on its payments? If a company has a strong balance sheet (healthy assets and manageable liabilities) and a history of good credit, it receives a high rating compared to a company with unmanageable liabilities and a poor credit history. The rating scale breaks down as follows:

AAA: High
AA: Very good
A: Good

BBB: Medium

BB: Low–Medium

B: Poor (bonds become "junk")

CCC: Worse (issuer may miss payments)

CC: Terrible (company usually misses payments)

C: Extremely Speculative (company has filed for bankruptcy or bankruptcy protection)

D: Default (company has been forced to liquidate)

Suspended rating: Company has defaulted and is in serious financial trouble

Banks are not allowed to invest in any company with a rating below BBB because of the higher risk of default on payments.

AAA bonds are much less risky than CCC bonds, which seem comparatively attractive as they promise a greater return than AAA. Because of the increased risk of default, companies with a CCC bond rate need to offer a greater return to incentivize investors to put their money at such great risk. However, if the company goes bankrupt, you'll have to wait until the lengthy legal battles are done before you get your money back, and you may only get a portion back after bankruptcy proceedings are complete. Most corporations work very hard to build and maintain a quality rating.

Strategies for Investing in Bonds

Avoid long-term bonds during periods of low interest rates: Bond prices perform inversely to interest rates. When interest rates are falling (or are expected to start falling), bond prices are rising. This means you'll be paying more by purchasing a long-term bond throughout periods of low interest; conversely you'll find cheaper bonds in a high-interest-rate environment.

Avoid junk bonds, especially in a down market: High yields don't always mean high returns or any form of security. Junk bonds might offer attractive returns, but they're issued by corporations that are in financial trouble. You might not get your money back, which makes the high interest rate a bad deal. Stick to well-known, high-quality bonds from organizations that can afford to pay interest in any type of market.

Buy high quality: The highest-quality corporate bonds tend to come from regulated industries such as banking, pipelines, utilities, and railways, which means they are fairly safe.

Diversify: Diversify your portfolio by buying bonds in many different industries with varying yields and maturity dates. Research and be aware of the callability features of bonds. (Sometimes bonds can be "called" by the issuer — basically purchased back by the issuer even though you have paid for them — and then reissued at different rates that are more favourable for the issuer and less favourable for you, the bond holder, which changes the terms of the bond.) Your original investment doesn't disappear, it just morphs into a new bond investment. Callable bonds can offer more attractive interest rates than bonds without this feature.

Interest reinvestment: Reinvest the interest you earn from the bond. For example, the bonds that I have in my portfolio are all compounding bonds. So, I don't need to do anything and the interest is ploughed right back into the bond, essentially growing my investment automatically.

Generate income: If you plan on not working for a while (because you're returning to school, raising a family, or taking early retirement), consider investing in simple interest bonds, because they can generate regular streams of income.

Safety: Timing the market is very difficult to do, but if you feel you want to take a chance, you can use bonds to support this initiative. If the economy appears to be heading into a recession, bonds can be a great place to store your investments, providing safety and security while they generate income. Additionally, their prices tend to increase as interest rates decrease and, throughout a recession, rates are typically cut to help stimulate growth in the economy.

If you don't know, use a bond fund: Bond mutual and index funds are available for investors who want to invest in bonds but haven't researched their decision. Professional fund managers select bonds with maturity dates and interest rates that, when pooled, should produce a solid return. As with all mutual and index funds, you pay a fee known as a management expense ratio (MER). If your fund returns 8 percent and the MER is 1 percent, your return will be 7 percent. Also consider that if you pay a broker to buy your bonds, you'll pay a percentage or flat fee to manage the purchase and sale. In both cases, you're paying for the services of professional management.

TREASURY BILLS

These are a short-term investment type issued by the federal government, and at times, the provinces. The T-bill is typically sold in larger denominations ($10,000 or more, depending on the length of the T-bill), but many financial institutions repackage T-bills so that you can buy them in smaller amounts, such as $5,000. A T-bill is sold to you at a discounted rate and purchased back by the issuer at full value.

The treasury bill is good for people who want to invest for 3, 6, or 12 months. You lend your money at a discount and the government "tops you up" when the money is due to be returned. For example, you might buy a T-bill for $9,500 that will be worth $10,000 on its maturity date. Your return is the difference between what you originally invested and the value at maturity. Besides cash, T-bills are the most liquid investment on the market and they can be bought and sold any time.

There is minimal risk involved with T-bills because they're government-issued, short-term lending investment; however, the returns are also minimal and therefore the T-bill won't give you significant long-term growth. A T-bill can be purchased through a broker, bank, or other financial institution.

Quite simply, T-bills are used primarily for short-term investments often leading up to a large purchase like a home or business. They offer excellent security of your principal while allowing you to make a decent rate of return given the short timeframe. Many large corporations use T-bills for their cash reserves until the funds are needed for a particular purpose like an acquisition of another company.

THE 411 ON STOCKS

Equity investments, such as stocks, mutual funds, index funds, and exchange-traded funds tend to be riskier than bonds, GICs, and T-bills; however, equities are more conducive to long-term growth.

There are two primary ways to make money in equities. First, there's appreciation in value (capital gains): selling the shares or units at a greater price than what you paid. Note that you must pay capital gains taxes on this appreciation. Second, you can collect dividends or distributions on the shares or units you own. As a reminder, dividends are a payment you collect quarterly for owning the shares. Distributions are essentially the same thing, but typically are paid out from units of a company that's legal structure is set up as a trust. For your portfolio to really grow, returns (dividends and distributions) should be reinvested.

> When you purchase stock, you own a piece of a company.

When you purchase stock, you own a piece of a company, which makes you a shareholder with voting rights. In other words, you literally have a vested interest in the company's success and therefore the value of your stock. You can buy stocks many ways: through an online or discount brokerage, a stockbroker on the stock exchange, directly from the company (this is uncommon), or through employee share-purchase programs.

Share prices of companies vary tremendously depending on how many shares are available on the market and the value of the company. There are penny stocks that sell for pennies and expensive stocks that fetch prices upwards of hundreds of dollars. The money you invest in any particular stock is never guaranteed, nor are you guaranteed any dividend payout. But even though there are no guaranteed returns, quality stocks have performed better overall than any other type of investment in the long run.

Companies and their stock fall into industry categories: consumer staples, consumer discretionary, diversified metals and mining, energy, financials, gold, health care, industrial, information technology, materials, real estate, telecommunications services, utilities, and income trusts. Each company's risk level, line of business, processes, management team, and finances are different from the next. As an investor, it's critical that you buy shares only in companies that fit your investment personality. You wouldn't want to buy stock in a high-risk mining company if you're a conservative investor, for example. Nor would you want to buy a "boring" bank stock if you're into high-risk, high-return resource-based companies.

Because no stock comes with a guaranteed rate of return, you'll want to do your very best to assess whether your stock pick is positioned for the performance you're hoping for given your investment needs. The next section will cover some stock research basics, but I recommend that you seek the advice of an investment adviser if and when you make a large share purchase, regardless of how well you've researched your hot stock.

How to Buy Stocks

Brokerage: You can purchase a stock (or bond) through a licensed investment professional who works at a stock brokerage firm or online through a discount brokerage. In the first instance, a full-service stockbroker (a.k.a., an investment adviser), charges a commission or fee for their advice. In the second, you invest based on your own research, without professional advice, saving fees in the process. Share purchase programs, which allow you to buy shares in regular installments, usually timed to your pay, are available through both styles of brokerage.

Direct: Shares can be purchased directly from the issuing company through a dividend reinvestment plan (DRIP) where your dividends are used to buy more shares. This is beneficial because it means your dividends are automatically reinvested rather than sitting in an account earning little to no interest. Some companies also allow employees to invest a portion of their pay directly into shares of the company.

How to Read Stock Details

If you've never looked at the stock section of a newspaper, it's time to have a peek. One of the best ways to learn about stocks is to track a few for fun. Pick your favourite companies and follow their performance for a few weeks. You can track stocks online through the major stock exchanges' websites — nyse.com or tmx.com — or through the newspaper. If you try the online route you can set up a mock portfolio through most brokerages (it's free!).

How to Evaluate a Stock

On its own, the price of a stock means nothing, but when you compare price, earnings, debt, industry, and other factors against other companies in the same peer group (sector, size, and line of business), you get a better picture of what the company is all about.

There are thousands of pieces of information about any one company. If you go to sedar.com, provided by the Canadian Securities Administration, you can pull up any public company's financial statements, annual reports, quarterly results, and any other material documents. In addition to a company's formal statements, news reports readily available on the web and analyst research available through your brokerage and sometimes on the web can provide further information.

Approaches to stock evaluation: There are two basic approaches to stock evaluation: fundamental and technical analysis. Fundamental analysis is based on the facts about a company, such as financial statements and earnings. The general economy and industry are also analyzed through fundamental analysis. Technical analysis is based on trading frequency, charts, patterns, trends, and all sorts of external factors that are believed to influence share price. Technical analysis appeals primarily to the mind of a trader (who is constantly looking for arbitrage [buying and selling] opportunities) versus the traditional investor's approach of fundamental analysis (based on facts and projected long-term growth).

I like to think of fundamental analysis as how you should determine *what* to buy and technical analysis as how you should determine *when* to buy. You can — and should — evaluate a stock based on both analytical approaches.

Price-earnings ratio: The first quick calculation you can run on a stock is called the price-earnings ratio (P/E ratio). It compares the price of the shares against the earnings per share. This information is available real-time on the stock exchanges' websites and through sedar.com. This ratio will give you a sense of what the company is earning. It's important to note that a company's projected future earnings, rather than its current earnings, are what really influence the stock price. The past is gone, and how a company plans to perform in the future drives its activities and share price. Here's what the P/E ratio looks like:

share price ÷ annual earnings per share = price-earnings ratio

Companies that are in their growth phase tend to have higher P/E ratios than companies that are matured or declining. This is because growing companies sell at a premium and there is great potential for stock appreciation. Big tech companies such as Tesla, Facebook, and Twitter all had high P/E ratios when they launched into the public market.

This ratio is fairly meaningless unless you compare it to companies in the same peer group and the market as a whole. Throughout the past century, North American stocks have averaged a P/E ratio of 15 times earnings. Standard P/E ratios are different for different industries.

Current ratio: To determine if a company is able to manage its debt load, calculate a current ratio. Read the company's financial statements and examine the company structure. This information is available on the company's website or through sedar.com. Both the financial statements and management analysis paint a picture of how fiscally responsible the company or business venture is. To figure out whether the business venture can afford to pay its short- and long-term debts, divide the company's current assets by its current liabilities to get the current ratio:

current assets ÷ current liabilities = current ratio

The higher the current ratio, the more likely it is that the company will be able to pay its bills in the short term. For many industries, if this number is less than 1.2, the company may be in short-term trouble.

Debt-to-equity ratio: Calculate a debt-to-equity ratio (divide total liabilities by total equity) to see if the company can afford to pay its debts in the long term:

total liabilities ÷ total equity = debt-to-equity ratio

In many industries, if the ratio is greater than two or three, the company may not be able to afford its debt payments in the long term.

It's important to note that it is okay for a corporation to have debt. *Carefully managed* debt enables a business to operate and grow in its line of business, which will potentially help generate positive returns for its shareholders.

Management, financials, competitors, and strategies: Determine whether a management team has the history and experience to carry a company through both challenging and good times. Read articles about the senior managers, examine the performance of the managers' past companies, and learn about their vision for the company, which will reveal future direction.

To invest wisely, you need to have a handle on a company's financial situation, its competitors (this will drive its likelihood of survival), and future direction. If you're looking for a summary of your target company's financial, strategic, competitive, and management information, get access to and read analyst research.

Get Investment Research

Financial analysts work for financial institutions involved in underwriting or bringing to market new securities like stocks and bonds for specific companies, and prepare reports on the companies that they cover. These highly paid and highly educated individuals make an assessment of the competitiveness of the company, report on a company's line of business, historical financials, share-price performance, earnings-per-share, capital-expenditure plans (the company's structure), debt position, and growth rates. The analyst also predicts the future of each of these factors. Analysts wrap up all of their research in a report indicating whether they believe investors should buy, hold, or sell. They also set a target — essentially an estimate — for the stock price. Their target price is not a guarantee!

Analyst research influences the price of stocks. It also influences the stocks that are recommended to you by a broker (especially if the research is coming from the same firm). Research is supposed to be an independent assessment of a company, but because institutions can sometimes be closely tied to the companies their research analysts cover, "independent" assessments can be somewhat influenced by existing relationships. I'd recommend gathering research from a few different sources, including an independent source that isn't involved in the underwriting of the company's security issues.

Generally speaking, if you have a brokerage account (whether it's with an investment adviser or you're managing it yourself), you have access to research produced by the firm where your account resides. Read this research as well as independent research on stocks from places such as:

- Globe Investor (globeinvestor.com)
- Canadian ShareOwner Investments (shareowner.com)

- CorporateInformation (corporateinformation.com)
- Value Line (valueline.com)
- Morningstar (morningstar.com or morningstar.ca)
- Yahoo! Finance (finance.yahoo.com)
- newratings.com (to find out if analysts have changed their stock rating)

When you are reading these reports you are looking for an assessment of where the company is heading. Is it on a path for growth or decline? Does it have a history of rewarding its shareholders with healthy dividends? Is its industry mature and declining or just ramping up? Obviously, you will want to invest in companies where your money is expected to grow.

Invest in companies where your money is expected to grow.

How Can You Tell When to Buy a Stock?

During the technology bubble (1999 to 2001), people invested based on hype rather than fact. Many companies announced advancements toward e-commerce and integration of the Internet into their business plans. With those announcements came soaring share prices; companies were trading on price-earnings ratios of 100 times their earnings. What was so incredibly frightening about the situation was the fact that many share prices were based purely on speculation. The industry inflated, reaching new share-price highs every day, until the bubble popped and the party was over, costing investors large portions of their portfolios.

Many investors invest in the market at the wrong time, which can cause them to lose money. It's really difficult to time the market and most people, even the professionals, don't always succeed. Buy low and sell high! When the market crashes and takes a significant hit, it's a good time to get in and buy good-quality investments aggressively.

Consider this: at the beginning of the 2008 financial crisis, the price of one Royal Bank share was more than $50, and by the end of 2008, amid the economic meltdown, Royal Bank shares were hovering at $30. The fundamentals of the company didn't change within that time frame; what changed was the economy as a whole.

Watch carefully for markets or sectors that reach new highs or new lows with great frequency. For example, if the oil and gas sector (or a particular stock within that sector) continues to reach new share-price highs, the industry could be reaching a new peak in prices, likely a result of higher commodity prices. This would be an expensive time to buy in. When that same sector reaches new lows over and over again, it would indicate a decline in price — a good time to buy. No one knows where the bottom or the top of the market is, but look for new highs and new lows to help understand if you're closer to the peak or the trough. Again, buying at the trough (lower price) and eventually selling your shares at or close to the peak (higher price) is a fundamental principle of making money in the stock market.

Should I Start Day Trading?

Day trading became very popular during the early 90s when a small few made big money fast by trading penny and technology stocks over the Internet during the day while sitting at home in their pajamas. For most, however, they were very far from becoming the next Wolf of Wall Street and lost a lot of money trying to trade stocks without any expertise. Unless you have inside information (which is illegal to trade on), most stock prices already reflect the information available in the marketplace. Therefore, there are few quick-buck bargain opportunities.

> Investing in stocks is a long-term game.

Investing in stocks is a long-term game. It can take a great deal of time for stocks to realize their full value potential or recover from losses, so hang on for the long haul. Investing successfully, like Warren Buffett, a legendary investor worth billions, requires a long-term perspective. Day trading focuses on short-term opportunities, which can have a great deal less return potential. Additionally, if you day trade, you'll pay higher commissions, higher taxes, and have less time for yourself because you'll be in front of the computer all the time.

If you really want to trade, train to become a professional trader at a legitimate marketing, trading, or brokerage firm.

Should I Buy Initial Public Offerings?

An initial public offering (IPO) occurs when a company offers new stock to the public. Facebook's IPO in 2012 was the biggest IPO in Internet history. The stock fell as soon as it opened, and share prices crashed more than 50 percent over the next couple of months. It took more than a year for the shares to trade above the $38 listing price, as there was concern earlier in 2013 that the company wouldn't make as much money from mobile ad revenue as it could from online ads. There was similar price volatility with Lululemon in 2007. Shares on the day of the IPO sold for $18 and closed at more than $28 on the same day. By January 2009, over a year later, the share price was less than $7. Yes, the market experienced a significant decline in value throughout that period, but even before the crash, Lululemon had lost a lot of value. In 2015, Lululemon shares climbed over $60 per share. Many other companies have experienced similar swings.

Most IPOs are presented to the market when times are good and when the company can get top dollar for its shares. This means the company makes more money and you buy more expensive shares.

Not all IPOs are bad. Some great companies issue IPOs that can be attractively (and realistically) priced. Just be cautious of IPOs that surface in a bull market; IPOs in a bear market can be better priced. On the whole, buy IPOs only if the stock fits with your overall long-term strategy (that is, you plan to hold on to it for a long time). So, for example, if you were a big believer in Facebook for the long term, early in 2016 your share price would be hovering around $100 per share. If you think that IPOs are for you, check with your discount or full-service broker to see whether you'd be allowed access to IPOs. Not everyone can gain access to IPOs through their brokerage account.

Hot Stocks, Penny Stocks, and Small Purchases

Overheated stocks are those that have gained a great deal of analyst, news, and investor attention. But, by the time the research reports are out and the newspapers have covered the company, the share price will have already reflected the news, and in a hyped-up market, that often translates into a higher share price. The market is very efficient, and so-called cheap buying opportunities are rare, especially for shares that have received a lot of media and financial analyst air time. Stocks may appear to be hot, but often by the time investors realize that, they've cooled down significantly.

Penny stocks are called that for a reason: they're not worth much, so don't buy them. Plus, there's often little to no information about the companies that offer them.

Finally, avoid small stock purchases, as you'll end up paying way too much in commissions for the sale. If you buy shares in small chunks, commissions will erode what you initially intended to put into your portfolio. Typically, discount brokerages charge anywhere from $8 to $30 per trade, and full-service brokers can charge a percentage of the trade or a flat fee, which is many times greater than through a discount broker. Generally, if you don't have at least $1,000 to invest, you shouldn't do a stock trade because of the fees.

MUTUAL FUNDS

A mutual fund is a group of stocks or bonds that combine to make a unit. When you buy one unit of a mutual fund, you're actually buying a little bit of every stock or bond within that unit. A professional fund manager chooses specific stocks and/or bonds that reflect a particular risk tolerance; the fund manager's primary goal is to outperform the market

The primary advantages of investing in a mutual fund are that you're able to easily achieve diversification because the fund invests in multiple stocks or bonds, and also that you benefit from professional money management. Think of it like this: if your mutual fund owns 25 stocks (evenly weighted) and one of the stocks goes broke, you lose 4 percent of the fund's value — one twenty-fifth of your investment. If you buy four stocks directly (evenly weighted) and one of them goes broke, you lose 25 percent or one-quarter of your portfolio. On the flip side, if one stock in a mutual fund soars in value, you'll experience less of a gain than you would if one of four individually owned stocks soared in value (in that case, you'd experience a much larger gain). Mutual funds diversify the risk of loss across many stocks.

Because mutual funds are directly exposed to the stock and bond markets, they are subjected to market volatility. When the markets are generally in a slump, your mutual funds will likely be in a slump as well; when the markets are hot, your funds will be too.

Mutual funds are categorized according to goals and risk tolerance. A high-risk fund focuses on holding stocks or bonds that have high risk and greater potential returns. Low-risk funds sacrifice returns for safety and therefore invest in stocks or bonds with low risk. There are thousands of different types of mutual funds available, such as growth, aggressive-growth, international, and income-producing.

> Mutual funds are an excellent way for new investors to get into the market.

Mutual funds are an excellent way for new investors to get into the market. Typically, the minimum lump-sum investment is $500, but these days, investors can start buying in at regular intervals for $50 or $100 per month. In fact, I started investing in mutual funds at the age of 14 and learned a great deal about investments from that experience.

Mutual Fund Cautions and Fees

Mutual funds are designed to be a long-term investment, so if you're hoping to hit a three-month home run, don't try it with this investment type. You should be invested for at least 7 to 10 years.

Also bear in mind that if a fund hasn't existed for at least 7 to 10 years, you're not going to get a full picture of its past performance. Look up the history of the fund manager's performance. Biographies are often posted by the fund manager's company, and independent ratings of fund managers can be found on the Internet. Check morningstar.ca or globeinvestor. com to see how funds and their managers are performing. If there's an emerging fund managed by seasoned professionals that you trust, then it's probably safe to consider it.

Mutual fund managers charge an operating fee known as an MER, which typically comes out of the fund itself, not your individual portfolio. This means the fee is shared among all the investors in the fund. MERs range between 1 to 2.5 percent. If the fund earns 8 percent and the MER is 1.5 percent, your return would be 6.5 percent.

In addition to the MER, some funds have front-end (when you buy) or back-end (when you sell) commissions. These commissions, also known as deferred sales charges, are paid to the broker selling the fund, not the fund manager. Some funds are no-load (no commission on the front or back), but read the fine print to ensure that you're not overpaying with other, hidden fees.

The key with any mutual fund portfolio is to invest in funds with low MERs and a history of strong returns relative to other funds in the category. The asset mix of every mutual fund is slightly different, but the goal of a mutual fund is to beat the market's performance. This can be tough to do if the MERs are too high and if the fund is over-diversified across multiple industries. When selecting a mutual fund, target an MER under 2 percent and look at the contents of the fund. You can see details of a fund's MER in the fund's prospectus (information circular), which can be downloaded from the fund's website or you can request a paper copy.

Index and Exchange-Traded Funds

Index and exchange-traded funds (ETFs) are used by the laziest investors … and more often than not, they perform better than mutual funds. Index funds mimic the overall performance of a particular index of stocks or bonds through electronic trading and portfolio management. For example, an index fund may follow the performance of the S&P 500 or the Dow Jones Industrial Average. The index fund holds the same stocks as that index and ensures the stocks are weighted as they are for that index as well. Investors then only need to follow the performance of the index to have an idea of how their own portfolio is performing.

An ETF is essentially the same as an index fund, but ETFs can target a very specific subset of the index, such as oil and gas companies worth less than $100 million, or an ETF can directly reflect the price of a commodity such as gold.

Both index and exchange-traded funds are managed by computers based on a specific investment policy. Index funds can be purchased directly through your bank. ETFs trade on the market like stocks.

The primary reason people like to invest in index funds and ETFs is that they won't underperform compared to the market because they are a representation of the market. On the other hand, the fund will never outperform the market either. Secondly, index funds and ETFs have lower MERs — 1.5 percent or lower — which makes them more affordable than mutual funds. Their MERs are lower because the funds are managed and rebalanced electronically according to an investment policy rather than actively managed by a well-paid fund manager. MERs on ETFs are even less expensive than index funds due to the limited trading and management involvement. Plus ETFs are not responsible for the fund's accounting (the brokerage is).

Index funds are typically better suited to passive investors, whereas ETFs are better for more seasoned investors who want to target a very specific subset of the market.

This table summarizes the key differences between funds:

MUTUAL, INDEX, AND EXCHANGE-TRADED FUNDS COMPARED

	Mutual funds	Index funds	Exchange-traded funds
Fees	Highest fees (MER) (1.5–2.5%)	Medium fees (0.5–1.5%)	Lowest fees (<0.5%)
Management	Active management	Passive management	Passive Management
Contents	Portfolio manager chooses individual stocks or bonds	Holds most stocks and bonds in a particular index	Broadest range of indexes (including higher risk)
Goal	Attempts to out-perform the market	Attempts to achieve market performance	Attempts to achieve market performance
Investor profile	Suited to passive investors	Suited to passive investors	Suited to active investors

Disclaimer: Mutual, index, and exchange-traded funds do not guarantee a rate of return.

Strategies with Mutual, Index, and Exchange-Traded Funds

Don't overdiversify: Funds are already a tool for diversification, so it is unwise to further diversify by buying into ten different funds, each charging an MER. If you choose a portfolio of funds, I suggest investing in a maximum of three funds, and if two funds contain the optimal allocation of companies within certain industries that match your investment personality, then choose the fund with the lower MER. If the fundamentals of the fund are different, choose the fund most aligned with your risk tolerance. Remember that over-diversification eats away at your ability to generate returns because of the fees.

Evaluate funds thoroughly: Given the choice between investing in funds with a 3-year history and a 10-year history, consider the 10-year-old fund as it gives you a more accurate reflection of the fund's performance (all else being equal).

Dollar-cost averaging: Contribute to the fund regularly through automatic banking withdrawals or payroll deductions in order to take advantage of an average price of the fund. For example, say you contribute $150 a month from your payroll deduction. Due to changes in the market, the cost of the fund units fluctuates — sometimes the cost may be low, sometimes high. By purchasing regularly, you're taking advantage of the fund's average cost, buying more units when the cost is low and fewer when the cost is high. And, regardless of the cost, you still experience the benefits of having annualized returns and distributions compounded.

Here's how it works: Let's say Tariq and Linda are investing in a mutual fund called "Big Canadian Stocks." The fund's average monthly prices are:

BIG CANADIAN STOCKS

	Average unit cost
January	$45.00
February	$55.00
March	$52.00
April	$48.00
May	$49.50
June	$53.00
July	$54.00
August	$53.00
September	$50.50
October	$51.00
November	$52.50
December	$44.00
Average	$50.63

If Tariq and Linda try to time the market and hold on to their investment dollars until they think the time is right, they might end up paying more or less than the average of $50.63. After watching the fund drop in value between February and March, perhaps they'll decide that it won't go any lower. Not only will they be wrong, but they'll end up paying more than the average cost over the year.

For new investors, funds make more sense than purchasing stocks or bonds directly. The risk of loss is lower and the formula for successful performance has been determined. It's turnkey. For more seasoned investors, it makes sense to invest directly into the stock or bond market. This will save money on fees but require more research.

SOCIALLY RESPONSIBLE INVESTING

Between the 1970s and 1990s, companies, pension funds, and individuals around the world stopped investing in South Africa. Since 1948, South Africa had been under apartheid, a system of legal racial segregation enforced by the ruling National Party. Apartheid encouraged other human-rights violations such as torture, censorship, political repression, exile, and detention without trial. To bring about change, outsiders divested their financial interests in the country. This forced financially struggling South African–based businesses (more than 75 percent of all that country's businesses) to negotiate for the dismantling of apartheid in 1994. In this case, socially responsible investing was used as a tool to create significant change in society, business, environment, and government.

Socially responsible investing has existed since the 1700s when religious organizations avoided "sinful" investments; for groups like the Quakers this meant insisting their members didn't participate in the slave trade. Modern ethical investing has become more complex because there are hundreds of investment products and fund managers directing their interests at a wide spectrum of social issues. With all the investment choices available, combined with the ever-increasing number of personal financial priorities, it's easy to forget that our investments can also make a difference while they make money. Socially responsible investing is about choosing to make a financial commitment to your social conscience; it goes beyond signing a petition. In a nutshell, it encompasses the protection of people, health, the environment, and human rights. Socially responsible investors typically avoid companies involved in such things as environmental degradation, actions that endanger public health and well-being, and human rights abuses. Many socially responsible fund managers, for example, avoid businesses involved in tobacco, alcohol, gambling, and the development of weaponry. "Green" investing focuses on environmental protection.

If this is an investment strategy you want to pursue, begin by examining your social values and what you feel is ethical and unethical. Follow your own guidelines to avoid investing in unethical companies and use your shareholder voting rights to make your voice heard.

> Socially responsible investing is about choosing to make a financial commitment to your social conscience.

Many socially responsible investors turn to professional money managers to rigorously divest, screen, and advocate on their behalf, and pay management fees for these managers to develop profitable, socially responsible investment strategies. Nearly every major financial institution offers socially responsible funds, which are listed on their respective websites.

The bad news with socially responsible investments is that they don't produce nearly the same returns as their unethical counterparts (funds that specifically invest in areas such as gambling, defence, tobacco, and alcohol). For decades, these types of investments, such as Barrier Fund, have significantly outperformed benchmarks such as the S&P 500 and *all* ethical funds.

The good news is that the Canadian socially responsible fund market has gained significant momentum and influence over the past few years, growing to well over $600 billion. This dramatic increase has been attributed to large pension funds adopting new social and environmental screening policies.

But the performance results are hit and miss, and many of these investments don't have more than 10 years' worth of data — an essential element when making an informed investment choice.

I'm not suggesting you avoid socially responsible investing because the returns are scattered; I'm encouraging a thoughtful consideration of investment history, management, and future direction. Socially responsible investing comes down to where you feel your money is most useful. Although apartheid is a thing of the past, many other despicable social structures and issues thrive today. You have the power to create significant change by following ethical guidelines to invest your money.

We know this market is growing and will surely become a seasoned and comparable performer as time passes.

DON'T STOP INVESTING

To really succeed at investing, think long-term growth suited to your risk profile. The more comfortable you are with your investment portfolio, the more likely you are to buy the right investments and stay invested. And staying invested is one of the key strategies to making money. Before I walk you through how to make money in stocks, here are some concluding pieces of investment advice:

1. **Start:** The sooner you start investing in your future, the more time you give compounded interest and reinvested returns to work their magic.
2. **Use helpful plans:** Investment plans like the RRSP and TFSA are designed to help you save more money by providing tax incentives. Company-sponsored savings and retirement plans are often a source of free money through matching programs. Always ensure that you're making the most of the savings and investment plans available to you.
3. **Contribute regularly:** Whether you're investing in a mutual fund or an individual stock, contribute to your investment plans regularly and ensure that you sign up for automatic dividend reinvestment programs (DRIPs).
4. **Asset allocation and diversification:** Ensure that what you invest in is suited to your long-term goals and investment risk profile. Proper asset allocation also helps to diversify your portfolio, thus reducing the risk of significant loss.
5. **Invest for the long term:** That way, you'll take full advantage of the growth potential within an investment.

6. **Monitor the commissions and fees you pay:** When you start investing, you'll have to pay transaction fees. Negotiate a better deal on all commissions, as they can seriously erode your portfolio (especially when you're starting out).

7. **Hire a smart investment adviser (a.k.a., a broker):** Chapter 11 (see page 169) has information on hiring an adviser.

8. **Don't stop investing:** Even if times get tough, ensure that you're saving money for your future, because no one else will do it for you.

Unemployment and other financial emergencies can knock your investing off track. Sometimes it means stopping your regular contributions or selling some of your investments. Once you're through this difficult period, pick up where you left off, and try to avoid the situation in the future by building up emergency funds.

CHAPTER 10
Invest Like a Pro 4.0: How to Make Money with Stocks

By now I'm sure you've got the sense that I'm not big on get-rich-quick schemes. The same applies to stock investing. I'm a believer in following strategies that are tried-and-true. You'll likely find as you read this chapter that some strategies sit better with you than others. Only go with the ones that feel right to you.

BUY-AND-HOLD AND VALUE INVESTING

Warren Buffett follows both the buy-and-hold and value-investing approaches to stock purchasing. He's been extremely successful in picking quality stocks that grow steadily in the long term. According to Buffett, "Only buy something that you'd be perfectly happy to hold if the market shut down for ten years."

The buy-and-hold approach to stock purchasing is fairly conservative in that the investor purchases very high-quality (non-risky) stocks and holds on to them for years. The investor makes money when the stock appreciates in value (producing capital gains when the stock is sold) and through dividends. Because there's little trading involved, the investor doesn't hop from investment to investment, paying high fees and not realizing the stock's full potential.

Buffett couples this with the more active and slightly less conservative value-investing approach. The same principles apply, but he takes it one step further. He buys quality stock that is beaten down or undervalued due to economic conditions or short-term hiccups. Another excellent Buffett quote that summarizes this principle is, "Look at market fluctuations as your friend rather than your enemy; profit from folly rather than participate in it."

Take the Ford Motor Company, as an example. For years leading up to the financial crisis that started in 2008, the company had lost its edge. It was heavily indebted and struggling against foreign imports. Once the financial crisis started to unfold, the share price of Ford tanked to its lowest point in history, and the company was preparing for bankruptcy. During that time, the American government stepped in to "bail" Ford out and help it get back on its feet. The reason for that was that Ford employs nearly one hundred thousand people right here in North America and is also a flagship industry — it's part of the backbone of the economy.

Today, Ford has reinvented itself and is a top-selling brand around the world. It took nearly losing its entire business to spark new leadership to take control of the brand and offer customers the latest technology, safety, reliability, and design.

Ford Motor is the perfect example of a company that experienced short-term pain, which value investors took advantage of when the company's stock was low. Ford investors in 2015–16 benefitted from long-term gain through a significantly higher stock price — over 12 times as valuable as it was at its low point during the financial crisis.

Again, the intention of a value investor isn't to make a quick buck; it's to buy and hold bargain-priced, high-quality stock. That makes this a fairly conservative strategy. The types of stock that can be described as "high quality" and "less risky" generally include banks, utilities, pipelines, and railways, which are all fairly conservative (and partially regulated) industries.

Value investing doesn't always work. There are times when companies or investments are in serious trouble and cannot recover. Stay away from those! Characteristics of such companies could include:

- Limited growth potential
- A dying industry (for example, bricks-and-mortar movie rental companies like Blockbuster)

- Unfavourable regulatory changes (for example, prohibiting the use of coal for electricity generation)
- Huge debts
- Massive controversy (for example, pharmaceuticals that have harmed people)

INVEST IN WHAT YOU KNOW

Peter Lynch, another well-known fund manager and author, believes you should invest only in what you know simply due to the fact that you'll be far more likely to conduct sufficient research into things that interest you. According to him, "The person that turns over the most rocks wins the game." The more you know, the better off you'll be at making investment decisions.

This strategy uses common sense to make investment decisions. If a business model is straightforward, how the business makes money — a key ingredient of growing a company — will make sense to you. You don't need to be a rocket scientist to figure this out either. Simply pay attention to brands and investments that are trending. Obviously, investing in a company that is growing will produce better returns than investing in one that is not.

If it is unclear to you how a company makes money, that company is generally not a good investment for you unless you're willing to put in the time to become more familiar with the company's business revenues.

Let's dive into an example. You may recall that in the 90s, the Gap was a hugely popular brand. Wearing Gap clothes was a fashion statement; the company was growing and so was its share price. In recent years, however, the value of the Gap brand has dropped significantly because the quality of merchandise has deteriorated and the company hasn't kept up with the latest trends. The Gap is an example of a company that most of us are familiar with but probably wouldn't invest in today because it is closing stores due to declining sales. In other words, the company isn't growing like it once was. To recover from this downward spiral, the Gap will have to reinvent itself and become a desirable brand once again.

You don't need to be a financial analyst to recognize this trend.

DIVIDEND STRATEGY

High-quality companies often pay dividends on their stock because they can afford to do so. This doesn't mean that their stock price is more expensive either. Recall that a dividend is a small reward (return) for holding the stock. You might receive a 1, 2, or 3 percent yield every quarter. A yield is the percentage of a dividend paid out in relation to the value of the share price. If you receive a $3 dividend payment in a year on a stock that is valued at $100 that indicates a dividend yield of 3 percent. The math is: $3 ÷ $100 = 3%.

> Receiving a dividend is like getting free money just for holding the stock.

I really like the concept of receiving a dividend because it is like getting free money or returns just for holding the stock. Dividend-paying companies tend to be more mature and can afford to pay a dividend, whereas growth companies tend to keep their money (by not paying a dividend) and reinvest it in the growth of the company.

The dividend-investing strategy is simply that you invest in companies that pay a healthy and growing dividend.

An increasing dividend is a good sign that the company is growing its income and the management team wants to attract great shareholders. To determine if an organization pays a high or low dividend, or if the underlying stock is healthy, simply compare the dividend yields among similar companies. This information is readily available on globeinvestor.com.

Be aware that a high dividend yield doesn't mean the underlying stock is healthy. If the stock has tanked but the dividend payout hasn't been lowered, the yield will appear deceivingly high. Consider both the yield and quality of the underlying stock.

Most financial experts recommend that you stay away from companies that are cutting dividends because this can indicate that a company is in trouble and can't afford to pay them (perhaps the company is in the throes of a major lawsuit that could lead to bankruptcy).

When the economy is in a recession, for example during an energy crisis, energy companies tend to cut their dividends because their income has gone down due to low commodity prices. Rather than pay out a dividend, the company chooses to reinvest the money into its internal growth. This can also occur if a company is changing strategy and needs to keep all of its income within the business for new growth opportunities.

DRIPs are dividend reinvestment programs and some of the best companies offer these. Rather than being paid out by an electronic deposit into your bank account, your dividends are automatically reinvested into more shares. DRIPs allow you to passively grow your portfolio without having to pony up more money to purchase more shares. So, your 100 shares can become 102 and then 105 … and all the while, you haven't had to lift a finger. The best part is that you then collect dividends not just on the original investment but also on your growing portfolio. Now that's compound interest and reinvested returns in action! To sign up for a DRIP, you simply need to check the box on your purchase agreement that asks if you would like to participate in the DRIP. DRIPs are not available for all stocks.

The dividend strategy isn't available just for investors investing directly into stocks. Dividend mutual, index, and exchange-traded funds are invested directly in stocks that pay high dividends. The returns from those stocks are then reinvested into the fund, providing the same compounding effect as a DRIP.

Generally speaking, large, healthy companies, known as "blue chip," are the ones that pay dividends. For example, a large resource-based company such as Suncor Energy or a technology company like Microsoft fall into the dividend-paying category. Dividends are subject to the company's board of director's approval. That means dividends can be cut if the board of directors believes that money should be used for other things.

When you invest in stocks that pay dividends, you benefit from the dividend tax credit. Go to the CRA website (cra-arc.gc.ca), select the appropriate language, Individuals and Families, Tax Returns, Completing, and then Deductions.

SECTOR ROTATION

Imagine you're walking down the street, minding your own business, when a stranger jumps out of an alley and kicks you. Initially, you'd feel defensive, then after a few seconds you'd feel aggressive — you *did* just get kicked by some random dude.

Sector rotation works in a similar way. When the markets are uncertain, you transition your portfolio into a defensive position. This means investing in tried-and-true, high-quality companies that have existed for many years while producing stable returns both in the form of share-price appreciation and dividend payments. I like to think of conservative investments as non-cyclical industries, such as banking, utilities, pipelines, and railways, which have low debt, stable returns, and intelligent management teams with successful track records.

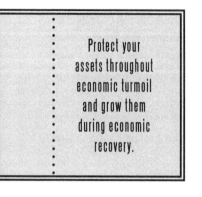

Protect your assets throughout economic turmoil and grow them during economic recovery.

When the markets start to bounce back, you rotate your portfolio into an aggressive position. This means buying more cyclical industries that tend to be commodity- or resource-based such as oil and gas, precious metals, or technology. These industries tend to be hit hardest during recessions but can produce significant returns when markets recover.

Sector rotation means you protect your assets throughout economic turmoil and grow them during economic recovery. There's growth through appreciation and capital gains when the markets are good, and protection (and dividends) when the markets are bad. You've probably guessed that this is a high-risk strategy for aggressive, growth-oriented investors. It can work if you're comfortable with the risk and have done ample research to support your positions. If you're a conservative investor, however, stay far away from this strategy.

If you do try sector rotation, be careful when selecting a cyclical stock in a volatile market because you never know if the market will continue to drop. Cyclical companies with ample cash and low debt tend to be the ones that survive rough markets; indeed, they may even be in a position to acquire struggling companies.

GROWTH STORIES

Stocks that are positioned for growth have the potential to produce high returns. Many are venture or start-up companies that have a new idea, product, or service. These companies are considered high risk, so they should be considered only by investors who fit a high-risk investment profile.

Growth strategies are based on the principle that small things grow bigger than big things, so small companies have huge potential to become big.

To profit from investing in small, growth-oriented companies, you absolutely *must* have research to support your decision, understand the business model, and be able to interpret financial statements properly. Small companies, for example, require the fiscal responsibility that comes from a strong management team, cash, and low debt, as these factors help fund research, development, marketing, distribution, and other important elements of running a business. Many technology companies fall into this category.

LEVERAGED INVESTING

Sometimes borrowing money to make money makes sense. It's called leveraging, and leveraged investing is a higher-risk endeavour than straight cash investing.

> Sometimes borrowing money to make money makes sense.

Let's say you've got $5,000 ready to invest. You've found a really great stock suited to your investment profile, and you're ready to call your broker and make the purchase. While on the phone with your broker, you learn that your stock, XYZ, is positioned for significant growth throughout the next three years. Your broker presents you with the research to help solidify your stock pick. Next, she asks if you'd like to buy more than $5,000 worth of shares using a secured investment loan at 7 percent.

Knowing that the stock is expected to grow at 10.5 percent each year over the next three-year period, she convinces you to borrow an additional $5,000 to put toward your stock purchase. You end up investing $10,000 and you have two years to pay back the investment loan.

Because you're expecting to earn a higher rate of return than you'll be spending on loan interest, you will make money if the stock grows at its expected rate. In fact, on the additional $5,000 that you borrowed, your relative overall rate of return after the three-year period will be 3.5 percent (10.5% – 7% = 3.5%). When you combine that with your original cash allotment of $5,000, on which you will have earned 10.5 percent, you end up making a very healthy return — far greater than the cost of borrowing.

Yes, you'd have to make monthly payments on the borrowed money. In this example, you'd likely be paying $225 a month toward your two-year loan. If you can afford to do this, you'll make additional returns because you'll have invested $10,000 and earned 10.5 percent (minus the interest on the $5,000 loan) versus earning 10.5 percent on $5,000. And if you invest this money in your RRSP of TFSA you receive tax advantages. The opposite is also true: borrowing to invest is far riskier than investing with cash because the value of your investments can fluctuate, but you're still going to be on the hook for paying back your investment loan. If debt and risk make you nervous, *don't* use leverage.

You should borrow to invest only if, first, you can afford to make the payments and, second, your expected rate of return is greater than the cost of borrowing. I also recommend leveraged investing only if you can afford to lose your money.

You can make money in stocks when you honour your risk tolerance, keep your fees low, take a long-term approach, and focus on quality investments; not junk. When you go off-track from your risk profile, and try to invest according to someone else's risk profile, that's when you'll run into trouble. Before you click the "buy" button in your investment account, ask yourself whether you'd be comfortable holding on to the investment for a long time. If not, it's probably not aligned with your risk profile.

CHAPTER 11
Design Your Master Money Plan

Money factors into the majority of your big life plans — marriage, home, career, family, retirement, travel — so it's important to have a financial plan. This is your life we're talking about!

Financial planning isn't about looking at our past, although we should always learn from the past. It's a collection of goals for your future and the steps you, as a couple, plan to take in order to reach them.

A written plan, which stands a better chance of success than one that is unwritten, can be as long or short or customized as you want. It's okay to be somewhat vague at first. You can refine and expand your plan as you gain a better understanding of what you want.

Eventually, your plan will include how much money you want to have saved when you retire, how many homes you want to own, where you'd like to travel, how many children you want to have, and other big goals you'd like to achieve. Next, you get a bit more specific about your dreams — what you want, when, how, and why. Then break your dreams into smaller steps. When you're ready, have a professional financial adviser or money coach review your plan. Last, you take action toward achieving your goals.

> It's important to have a financial plan. This is your life we're talking about!

Planning ahead can be daunting at first, but don't worry; this chapter will help you and your honey build a rock-solid financial plan.

PRINCIPLES OF FINANCIAL PLANNING

Bradley and Jamie are married and in their early 30s. Over the past three years, since forming a permanent household, they've set very loose verbal financial goals and have made some progress toward them.

But every year when the cold winter rolls in, they cave in to the temptation of taking an unplanned, expensive, warm winter holiday costing an average of $5,000. This action continues to put them back financially because less of their money goes toward reducing their debt and growing their savings for retirement.

Frustrated because they don't seem to be making progress, Bradley and Jamie decide to write a five-year financial plan, review it with their money coach, and sign the physical document as a commitment to keep each other accountable to their plan.

Now every month they track their progress, discuss any issues, and take action toward correcting areas of concern. They can still afford their lifestyle, but they don't let trips and other luxuries derail their important financial goals.

Your financial plan consists of three main components. The first is a set of goals you want to work toward. The second is your projected income growth, which will support your goals. The third is your projected net worth, which is the number we want to focus on growing through the financial-planning process.

These three components are accompanied by "make it happen" strategies.

Income Growth

Jamie, a dental assistant, is due for a raise in the next few years. Bradley wants to stop practising massage therapy in a clinic and start his own small business providing massage to people in-home. Together they expect their incomes to grow by approximately 3.5 percent every year. The only disruption in income will occur in three years, when they plan to have a baby; Jamie's income will drop while on parental leave.

Bradley and Jamie's financial plan is below.

BRADLEY AND JAMIE'S FIVE-YEAR FINANCIAL PLAN

Goals

- Financial:
    - Grow our investments to $100,000.
    - Save a down payment.
    - Become debt-free, other than the mortgage.
- Personal:
    - Start a family.
    - Buy a home valued at $450,000.
- Professional:
    - Jamie to get a promotion.
    - Bradley to start his own business.

BRADLEY AND JAMIE'S INCOME GROWTH

	Year 1	Year 2	Year 3	Year 4	Year 5
Bradley's income	$55,000	$56,925	$58,917	$60,979	$63,114
Jamie's income	$45,000	$46,575	$21,500*	$48,205	$49,892
Total household income	$100,000	$103,500	$80,417	$109,185	$113,006

* parental leave

Net Worth

Today Bradley and Jamie's net worth is $50,000. Their goal is to grow their net worth to just over $150,000 within five years. They will do this by growing their savings for retirement, purchasing a home, and eliminating their non-mortgage debts.

BRADLEY AND JAMIE'S NET WORTH

	Current Value	Year 1	Year 2	Year 3	Year 4	Year 5
Assets						
Bradley's RRSP	$9,000	$11,000	$13,000	$15,000	$17,000	$19,000
Jamie's RRSP	$12,000	$14,000	$16,000	$18,000	$20,000	$22,000
Jamie's defined contribution plan	$30,000	$35,000	$40,000	$45,000	$50,000	$55,000
Bradley's TFSA (down payment)	$7,500	$12,500	$17,500	$22,500	$0	0
Jamie's TFSA (down payment)	$7,500	$12,500	$17,500	$22,500	$0	$0
House	n/a	n/a	n/a	n/a	$450,000	$450,000
Total assets	**$66,000**	**$85,000**	**$104,000**	**$123,000**	**$537,000**	**$546,000**
Liabilities						
Bradley's student loan	$6,000	$4,000	$2,000	$0	$0	$0
Car loan	$8,000	$5,000	$2,000	$0	$0	$0
Line of credit	$2,000	$0	$0	$0	$0	$0
Mortgage	n/a	n/a	n/a	n/a	$405,000	$390,000
Total liabilities	**$16,000**	**$9,000**	**$4,000**	**$0**	**$405,000**	**$390,000**
Net worth (assets – liabilities)	**$50,000**	**$76,000**	**$100,000**	**$123,000**	**$132,000**	**$156,000**

MAKE-IT-HAPPEN STRATEGIES

- Cut out any unnecessary spending on restaurants and reduce the entertainment and travel budget.
- Sublet the basement of their rented house.
- Side hustle — Bradley and Jamie will get additional work (freelance or part-time jobs).
- Reinvest tax refunds into the down-payment TFSAs.
- Avoid any additional debt.

STEPS TO CREATING A KICK-ASS FINANCIAL PLAN

These are the financial planning steps that we will discuss in this section:

- Organizing your financial records
- Setting goals for the future
- Increasing your income
- Tracking your net worth
- Creating a budget to support your plan
- Committing to your plan and evaluating your progress
- Protecting what you've worked so hard to earn
- Finding a great financial adviser or money coach

Organizing Your Financial Records

Organization is the key to building a successful financial plan. In order to create a solid financial plan, you need to know the status of your investments, loans, mortgages, home value, insurance policies, wills, deeds, tax returns, pay stubs, and bank accounts.

If you haven't already done so, you'll want to create files — paper or electronic or both — for all of these important financial records. As you start to execute your financial plan, you'll need to refer to these files to track your net-worth progress and to have informed discussions with your financial adviser or money coach.

Setting Goals for the Future

A great financial plan starts with dreaming. Your dreams will drive your goals and choices around lifestyle, financial priorities, and budget. Ultimately, your dreams will lead you to a particular future such as a comfortable retirement, the ability to open a small business, pass wealth on to your children, or trade in your house and car to travel the world.

> The purpose of a financial plan is to achieve financial freedom.

The purpose of a financial plan is to achieve financial freedom. What financial freedom means to you isn't necessarily the same as what it means to someone else — and that's okay! This is your future, no one else's. What does financial freedom look like to you?

Just like Bradley and Jamie, your financial plan should contain goals for the three pillars of your life — financial, personal, and professional. Your financial goals, for example, would include your savings, investments, and debt repayment. Your personal goals would include real estate, family, travel, and entertainment. Your professional goals would include raises, promotions, or starting a business.

What are your financial, personal, and professional goals?

Increasing Your Income

Incomes traditionally rise over the course of your career. You'll advance in your skills and responsibilities and should receive compensation that matches those advancements. As part of your financial plan, you'll want to take into account future plans for increasing your income, as well as the timeline for those projected changes.

There are three primary ways to increase your income, and you'll want to determine which are most appropriate:

- Through raises and promotions from traditional employment (either salaried or hourly) with an employer
- By starting and growing a profitable business
- By producing income from your investments such as stocks, bonds, mutual funds, and real estate

Sometimes you might receive irregular or unexpected income. There may be circumstances in the future when you find yourself with a lump sum of money like an inheritance, a bonus from work, an increase in property value, or a large tax refund. Though you may not know when or if you will receive lump sums of additional income, you can always plan for how you would use that money if you did. For example, perhaps you would put 75 percent toward your retirement account and the other 25 percent toward paying off debt.

How do you plan to grow your income?

Tracking Your Net Worth

Growing your net worth is the foundation of any solid financial plan, so let the measure of your personal net worth drive the actions you will take to achieve your financial goals. As a reminder, to increase your net worth you must reduce your liabilities and build your assets.

Your financial plan might be to increase your net worth by $5,000 this year by purchasing investments and making payments on your car loan. Next year, you might want to increase your net worth by another $6,000. The key idea is that you want to grow your net worth each year.

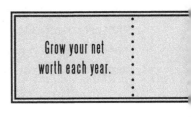
Grow your net worth each year.

In Bradley and Jamie's case, they plan to triple their net worth over five years through aggressive debt reduction and asset growth. They are on a mission to simplify their finances by eliminating all non-mortgage debt and growing their retirement savings. Their specific make-it-happen strategies are not complex and, more important, are realistic.

Congratulations! You've just worked through the foundation of your financial plan. Now you and your partner can create a simple financial plan using Bradley and Jamie as a template. Don't worry if your goals change. You can pop back into this document and adjust your plan when you need to. I recommend sticking to a five-year timeframe. Anything longer is hard to plan due to many changing variables.

Creating a Budget to Support Your Plan

Now that you've drafted your financial plan, you must align your budget with it. Remember, your budget lists your income and expenses. When expenses are subtracted from your income, that is what you have left over, or your bottom line. Your budget is a starting point for determining how you will reach your financial goals because it allows you to track and assess your income and spending. Your budget needs to accommodate your goals, income, and net-worth growth.

Using your expected income, and taking into account your goals for the future, extend your budget over a five-year period. This can be done by month for the current year, then by year for future years. Head back to chapter 3 for a budget refresher when you need it.

If you plan to grow your net worth by contributing $12,000 to your investments in each year of your financial plan, you'll need to find approximately $1,000 per month in your budget for these investment contributions. Or you may wish to pay an extra $6,000 on your mortgage this year, which means you'll have to review this year's budget to determine how you can afford to make that extra payment. Perhaps you'll pay an extra $500 per month. Or you may use your tax refund or bonus from work to make a lump-sum payment. The idea here is that your budget should be designed to help you achieve your goals.

Committing to Your Plan and Evaluating Your Progress

Building your net worth is hard work. But watching your net worth grow is really awesome: $10,000 to $30,000 to $70,000 to $250,000. It makes all the hard work seem worth it when you can quantify your progress. The best way to track your progress is through your net-worth spreadsheet.

By regularly reviewing your important financial statements, if you see that something is getting off track, you can address it quickly. For example, if you didn't make enough of an RRSP contribution in Year 1 of your plan, you can rectify the situation throughout Year 2.

I recommend that you review your financial plan every six months to see that you're on track to achieve your goals.

Protecting What You've Worked So Hard to Earn

You've spent all this time and energy establishing your financial plan. But what about protecting what you've worked so hard to build?

Though it's not pleasant to think about illness, disease, death, disability, and other awful events, catastrophes can happen and you need to be equipped with the right life and disability insurance along with a comprehensive will to get you through. Spending the time now to get your insurance coverage properly organized and your will established will allow you to rest easy in the event something terrible happens to you or your family.

Disability and Life Insurance

Disability and life insurance are designed to protect your future income-earning ability and estate value. Without these types of insurance, you and your family could experience major financial catastrophe if you end up unable to work or deceased.

You should have life insurance if your family is financially dependent on you. You're less likely to need life insurance if you are single or have buckets of money that you'll be leaving for them.

Even if you are dependent on your partner's income and they are not dependent on yours, it's still a good idea to have life insurance on both your lives. Think of it this way: if you have no income because you are staying at home to look after your children and you die, your family will no longer have a caregiver. Your partner will be forced to find another, which costs money.

There are two categories of life insurance: cash-value (such as whole, variable, or universal life) and term life. We'll discuss these now.

Cash-value policies have a savings component to them. You pay a premium, part of which goes into a savings plan. If you exit the plan, you keep the savings that you've built up. The benefit of having this type of policy is that you will definitely have a guaranteed amount of money set aside in savings *and* your annual premium is set. The alternative to this plan, term life insurance, doesn't provide that type of savings security. With term life, if you stop paying your premium, you are no longer covered and you have no savings.

Cash-value plans do have a downside. There's a big price tag associated with that savings feature. The long-term cost of having a cash-value life insurance policy is between 5 and 10 times higher than a term life policy.

For some people, cash-value policies make sense. If you don't mind paying for extra security, it's a nice way to have insurance coverage and build savings at the same time.

Some people feel better that their insurance premiums are at least going toward some savings rather than just toward premiums. But always remember that a cash-value policy is first and foremost a life insurance policy, not a retirement savings plan. Many cash-value policyholders do not select adequate coverage because they are too focused on how much money they can save up using the savings feature of the cash-value plan, putting themselves at risk. Get the right amount of life insurance coverage and don't let the savings component distract you.

Term life policies are pretty straightforward: you pay an annual premium for a pre-set amount of life insurance. If you die, your beneficiaries collect that predetermined amount. If you don't die during the term of your policy, your premium is gone. There is no savings feature. Term policies have adjustable premiums and terms (between 5 and 20 years) because your risk of dying increases as time passes. You pay the same premium for that term until it is adjusted to a different term. The cost of a term policy, in the long run, is far less than that of a cash-value policy.

The biggest problem with term policies is that the premium increases as you age. The increase tends to discourage individuals from renewing their plan, and once you stop contributing, your insurance coverage ends, so those who don't renew end up not being covered by any type of insurance.

If both of you are working, a good rule of thumb when buying life insurance is to have enough coverage to replace anywhere from 5 to 10 years' worth of your respective salaries. If one partner earns $100,000 annually, 5 years of income would equate to $500,000 of life insurance and 10 years would equate to $1 million of life insurance.

If you are a sole income provider, life insurance should comprise at least 70 to 75 percent of the replacement value of your annual income for the number of years you plan on continuing to work.

For example, if you earn $50,000 annually; you're 35 years old and want to work for 30 more years. Take $50,000 × 75% × 30 years = $1.1 million in coverage.

Ultimately, you want enough life insurance coverage to ensure that your family is taken care of within reason. Speak to an insurance professional about your situation.

Disability insurance is often overlooked because people simply don't perceive the risk of becoming disabled. But you're more likely to become disabled than you are to die. If you become disabled, you'll need to have enough time and money to supplement your income or figure out how to get another source of income, especially if you're the primary income earner.

Jose, a 25-year-old architect, for example, experienced an unfortunate accident that left him permanently blind. He relied on his disability insurance for two years to support his financial needs while he retrained to become a massage therapist.

Talk to your insurance agent about getting enough disability insurance in the event you wouldn't be able to work. It's in your best interest to fully understand the policy and its cancellation, renewal, waiting periods, and, most important, its definition of a disability.

If you have a traditional employer, check out your company and group insurance plans through work because they may include excellent life and disability insurance programs.

There are two primary ways to save money on life and disability insurance premiums. The first is to take advantage of discounts offered by your employer's group plans, your alumni association, or consumer associations. The second way to save is to use an insurance broker. An insurance broker can solicit plans that are suitable for you and the best prices from multiple insurance providers. A good insurance broker will be upfront about fees and commissions and be willing to spend time with you evaluating your situation so that you can select the best coverage. Before you hire a broker, get referrals from friends and family.

Wills

Death can't be avoided, so you need to plan for the inevitable. Having your financial house in order means being organized so that your loved ones can navigate through difficult times as easily as possible. Without a will, your spouse, partner, and/or executor is left working with the government to disperse your assets and manage your liabilities.

A will ensures that your wishes are honoured when you die. It is a legal document specifying what you'd like done with your assets and other belongings.

Estate planning experts recommend that you have a will prepared if you're over 21 years old, are married or living common-law, have dependants or children (biological or adopted), or have acquired assets such as an RRSP or a home, or liabilities such as debts.

A will is an opportunity to designate the people or organizations you want to receive your property. It allows you to specify who you would like to care for your children should their other parent also be unable to care for them. If, for example, you don't have a will in which you have appointed a guardian and you die, the courts and social service agencies will determine who will raise your children. Lastly, you can select an executor of the estate to carry out the wishes expressed in your will.

And whether you have children or not, without a will provincial law determines how your property will be distributed through a probate process. This process can be costly, time-consuming, and incredibly frustrating.

To draw up a will, you can see a lawyer or create one yourself. If you decide to draw up a will on your own, use a high-quality will-preparation software program. Once you've prepared your will, it's still wise to have a lawyer review it. If the document is satisfactory, it should be signed by you and notarized by a lawyer or notary public.

You should include an up-to-date list of all your assets and liabilities with your will. All debts must be paid after your death and what's left over, minus legal and other estate management fees, is distributed to your beneficiaries. Administratively, it's much easier for your executor to honour your wishes if he or she has a clear view of the situation.

Review your will at least every two years and update it as your personal situation changes — through marriage, children, divorce, death, a move to a new province or country, or if you want to change your beneficiaries, guardian, or executor.

Finding a Great Financial Adviser or Money Coach

It's a smart idea to involve an expert in your financial planning. A financial adviser through your bank or independent money coach can give you an objective opinion based on research from reliable sources. They can assist couples in navigating through financial disagreements while prioritizing and setting realistic goals. They can help you implement the right strategies to deal with any problems that might surface along the way.

In addition to all these benefits, a financial adviser or money coach can provide comprehensive advice aimed at optimizing your investment returns, ensuring that you have the right insurance coverage, reducing taxes, decreasing debt, building savings and investments, and helping plan your estate.

If you're going to hire an adviser or money coach, get referrals from people you trust. Then interview a few to see if you like them and to get a sense of whether they're being honest and realistic. Next, ensure that each is qualified. Check their education and their personal reputation plus the reputation of the company they work for.

Have each candidate prepare an analysis of your current financial plan (the one you've just drafted while reading this chapter) and see which adviser or money coach's recommendations are most aligned with your goals.

Many investment and financial advisers earn money through a combination of some of the following: an hourly rate, a commission, a percentage of assets managed, and maintenance and transaction fees. A good adviser will always be upfront about the costs and benefits of doing business. A money coach typically earns money through an hourly rate.

If you don't want to pay advisory fees, check out what's available through your local financial institution. Banks sometimes provide in-house advisers free of charge, though they tend to sell proprietary products (ones that are managed by the bank) like mutual funds or mortgages.

If you have a healthy amount of investments, you can also explore higher-end investment advisory services, which cost money. In all cases, advisers that manage investments must be licensed through the Investment Industry Regulatory Organization of Canada.

Bring this book with you when you go in to interview your adviser. Ask them the following:

- What are your credentials?
- Can I check your references?
- What is your philosophy about managing or advising me on my money? Is it aligned with my needs?
- How many times will you call me each year? How many times can I call you?
- Will you call me each and every time we make a change to my accounts, or can you act on my behalf (also known as having discretionary privileges)?
- If I have a problem with you, who can I call?
- What are your fees?
- Will you review and/or continue to develop my financial plan?

Your financial plan is a master plan for your money. You design it. You make it happen.

Conclusion

Look, I get that financial planning might seem overwhelming and isn't everyone's idea of a good time, but hopefully, after having read this book, it all seems a bit less daunting. Keep in mind those seven smart steps to building wealth together:

1. Get on the same page
2. Scrap your emotions and sort out your accounts
3. Curb overspending
4. Get the hell out of debt
5. Own the walls you live in
6. Invest like a pro
7. Design your money master plan

And follow them. You, your relationship, and your future will be better for it.

CHANGE YOUR MINDSET ...

The formula for staying poor is simple:

1. Ruminate over financial mistakes from the past
2. Compare yourself to others
3. Blame your circumstance on other people (including your partner) and situations that you couldn't control

The biggest financial obstacles for couples aren't their actual finances, but their mindsets. A fascination with the past prevents even the smartest couples from achieving their full potential — financial, personal, and professional. You might blame that stingy boss who would never give you a raise, or that ex-spouse who wouldn't pay their fair share of child support. Sure there will have been challenges along the way, but couples need to own up to their financial reality.

Compounding this focus on the past, is a torturous pattern of trying to keep up with the Joneses because "we deserve it." You know these people. You may be one. I was one once. In late 2015, a 45-year-old woman came into my office seething with anger because her ex-husband was a deadbeat and left her with a mountain of credit card debt ... eight years prior! Rather than owning up to her financial reality, she'd kept up "appearances" and buried herself further in debt. The past trapped her. She needed to stop obsessing about her ex, examine her own behaviour, and deal with the reality she was living in now.

... AND FOCUS ON SOLUTIONS

As couples we spend a lot of time looking in the rear-view mirror hoping that it will teach us something about the financial road ahead. But sadly, we miss simply being present in today — taking in what's happening right here and right now. Extraordinary things come out of many "todays" layered together when they are pointed in the direction you want your life and finances to head. If you want to be rich — and when I say that I mean that you would like to be truly satisfied with your financial, personal, and professional life — then take stock of where you and your money are today. This can be as simple as calculating your net worth, setting a realistic goal to grow it, and working to change one bad financial habit at a time. Make a resolution with your partner to stop arguing about who is responsible for the financial situation you're in, and focus instead on solutions.

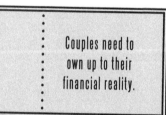

Couples need to own up to their financial reality.

Some of the most amazing financial progress I've seen is with couples starting from ground zero — they didn't even have two nickels to rub together, but their commitment to a better financial future was centred on making the best financial choices possible with what they had every day … and they were quick to halt bad financial habits.

If you're ready to transform your finances and your relationship, choose the formula for getting rich:

1. Put past financial mistakes in their place — behind you
2. Get real with your financial reality
3. Point every decision you make toward achieving your financial, personal, and professional potential

A happy relationship requires trust, communication, and love through thick and thin. As you work to strengthen your bond, remember that financial compatibility is a core ingredient of the glue that binds the two of you together. Do your best to ensure your financial decisions uplift each other and help build your future.

Index

By the Same Author

From the author of the National Bestseller
Well Heeled: The Smart Girl's Guide to Getting Rich

Lesley-Anne Scorgie

RICH by
THIRTY

Your Guide to Financial Success
2nd Edition

RICH BY THIRTY
Lesley-Anne Scorgie

Think you can't be rich by thirty? Think again!

The earlier you make savvy decisions with your finances, the more successful you can be because time is on your side. And you don't need thousands of dollars or a hefty inheritance to get started. In fact, most young millionaires began by saving a few dollars each week — the cost of a bottle of water or a drop-in fitness class.

As a financially savvy young person, you will have the ability to choose the direction of your future rather than having to accept what life throws your way — and that's valuable because having choices will help you create a happy life.

Forget about being broke! This guide will help you grow your money and empower you to create an awesome, and affordable, future for yourself.

WELL-HEELED
Lesley-Anne Scorgie

Whether you're financially maxed out or rolling in hundred-dollar bills, if you want to be rich, *Well-Heeled* is for you!

As a financially independent young woman, you will have the ability to determine the direction of your career and life path, allowing you to reach your full financial potential.

So if you're ready to make more money, live debt free, and build a nest egg that can support an awesome future — one that's designed by you and includes the splash, the chic, and the fun — check out *Well-Heeled*.

This guide will pump up your bank account and empower you to do and be whatever you want in life. Don't wait for success to come calling — start today!

Of Related Interest

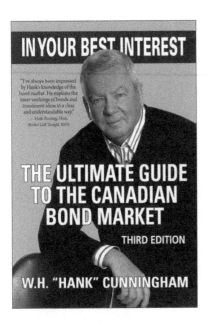

IN YOUR BEST INTEREST

W.H. "Hank" Cunningham

With more than one trillion dollars in bonds outstanding, the Canadian fixed income market is enormous. In fact, its daily trading volume is almost five times that of the equity markets. Yet investors and even many financial advisors know little about it.

In Your Best Interest demystifies the retail fixed-income market, from the basics of a bond to the various products available and a full discussion of the mathematics of bonds and the bond market. It also provides useful tips on selecting the right adviser. This third edition of *In Your Best Interest* gives you the tools to meet your income and retirement needs by making the retail fixed-income market less expensive, more accessible, and more efficient.